BEHIND THE VELVET ROPE

CONFESSIONS OF A GOSSIP COLUMNIST

By Jason O'Callaghan

First published in Ireland by Jason O'Callaghan
Publishers Prefix 0-9550889
93 Cherryfield Road, Walkinstown, Dublin 12.
www.theirishratpack.com

ISBN 0-9550889-0-9

Author's photograph by Barry McCall
A CIP catalogue record for this book is available from the British Library
Printed by Printing Solved, 96 The Village, Porterstown, Dublin 15
Cover Design by Pen and Pixel Design, Dublin
(contact@penandpixeldesign.com)

If errors occur with missing photo credits please contact the publishers to provide them with updates for future editions.

In memory of my mother

Geraldine Chute O'Callaghan

"Love your enemies
Just in Case your friends
Turn out to be a bunch of bastards"

R.A. DICKSON

WITH THANKS

To everyone in every publication I have worked on: *The Echo, The Star,* the *Sunday Independent, The Mirror,* the *Sunday World, U* magazine, *Food & Wine* magazine, *WHO* magazine, *Ireland on Sunday* and the *Evening Herald.*

To Dennis Desmond, Peter Aiken and Mick Roche for their advice and guidance. To my late mother, who is forever in my heart. To Etain Boyd, the best friend anyone could ask for and the one who has had to put up with me waffling on about this book for nearly a year.

Thanks to Anita Loughran in Bank of Ireland; Taragh Loughrey Grant at FM104; Audio Networks; Amanda Brunker; Mick Heaney in *The Sunday Times*; Larissa Nolan and Bob Conway in East Coast Radio; Colm Hayes in FM104; Mick Devine, Paul Drury, John Kierns, Dave O'Connell, Bernard Phelan and Ger Colleran; Paul Martin (you're still Number Two); Phil Cawley at Today FM; Dave Fanning and Jim Lockhart at 2FM; Gay Byrne and Pat Kenny; PJ Gibbons, Q102; Ray in Showbiz Ireland; Mike Hogan; Shay Healy; Swan O'Sullivan accountants; Chris Barry, Tom Cole, Anna Lavery and everyone at Ballyfermot Senior College. A special thanks to my aunt Anne Chute in France, whose phone call changed my life.

To Anne Harris and Aengus Fanning thanks for giving me a chance.

"Everything I did in my life that was worthwhile, I caught hell for."

EARL WARREN

ABOUT THE AUTHOR

Jason O'Callaghan was born in Tralee, Country Kerry, in 1973 and moved to Dublin just after his first birthday. He was raised in the Dublin suburb of Walkinstown and attended Saint Damien's National Boys primary school in Crumlin before attending secondary school at Synge Street CBS in Dublin's inner city.

He spent two years in the Dublin College of Catering and served his apprenticeship as a professional waiter. At 19 he attended Crumlin Business College to study for a diploma in Sales and Marketing but left just before his exams to live in Paris where he worked as part of the opening crew in Disneyland.

At 22 he went to work as a station head waiter aboard the world famous QE2 cruise liner before returning to college in 1996 to study journalism in Ballyfermot Senior College in Dublin.

He now lives between his homes in Cannes and Dublin performing with his band The Irish Rat Pack. He has just recorded his first solo album *Velvet Swing*. For more information see www.theirishratpack.com.

PRELUDE

This book is not aimed at ruining anyone's life. It's a true story of my life and shows how anyone can change their destiny. I am grateful to everyone who has helped me over the years and even though I may write some things about you in this book that you may not like, they are in the past. So, remember it's the future that matters. This book closes a massive chapter in my life and I hope each reader enjoys reading how a young waiter from Dublin ducked and dived his way behind the velvet rope and into a world of rock stars, film premiers and celebrity scandal.

Jason O'Callaghan
Cannes
July 2005

BEHIND THE VELVET ROPE

CONFESSIONS OF A GOSSIP COLUMIST

CONTENTS

Chapter 1: How it came to be (1996)

Chapter 2: You can't write, you can't spell, and you'll go a long way (1997)

Chapter 3: The Boyzone and Spice Girl years (January–June 1998)

Chapter 4: Who the hell is Colin Farrell? (July–December 1998)

Chapter 5: Hello Mr Willis (January–June 1999)

Chapter 6: Goodbye Terry, hello Posh (July–August 1999)

Chapter 7: The birth of "The Double Edge" (September–December 1999)

Chapter 8: A new millennium — private jets and supermodels (January–June 2000)

Chapter 9: Would you like to dance, Mr Flatley? (July–December 2000)

Chapter 10: The incident of the glass and the model (January–June 2001)

Chapter 11: Breaking into the Bond wedding (July–December 2001)

Chapter 12: McFadden the liar (January–June 2002)

Chapter 13: Not all fun and games (July–December 2002)

Chapter 14: Crossing Jordan (January–June 2003)

Chapter 15: The last days of 'The Double Edge' (July–October 2003)

Chapter 16: The end of an era (2003/2004)

Chapter 17: Conclusion

"What's money?
A man is a success if he gets up in the morning and goes to bed at night and in between does what he wants to do"

BOB DYLAN

CHAPTER 1

HOW IT CAME TO BE

(1996)

In uniform aboard the QE2-1995

Before I dive into tales of world-famous rock stars, actors, models and politicians let me tell you how a chancer from Dublin took on Ireland's social and showbiz elite and got into a position that really pissed them off beyond belief.

For nearly 20 years Terry Keane was Ireland's most feared and most dangerous gossip columnist. I, however, was a completely unknown waiter. The only danger I represented to anyone was if I spilt their soup on them.

Terry's name would strike terror into the hearts of the country's social elite. Millionaire businessmen, models, actors, singers, politicians and just about anyone in the public eye were all scared of her and what her column might say about them. The most fear I could strike into people's hearts was that I would get their orders wrong.

She commanded the ear of some of the country's most powerful people, including Charles J. Haughey who was Taoiseach for much of the time when she was queen of the social elite. I commanded the ear of a few workers in the QE2's crew mess.

She had an audience of over one million people who religiously read her weekly social diary in the *Sunday Independent*. The paper was then, and still is, Ireland's biggest-selling newspaper. I probably served lunch to as many guests.

So you can see why the story of how I took over Terry's job within one year of graduating from college — and why so many people have tried to stop me from telling it — would be an interesting one.

TRADING PLACES

In 1996 Terry was more powerful than ever. Unbeknownst to anybody, though, things were soon to change, and not just for Terry. The bombshell that was coming would affect the *Sunday Independent*, the former Taoiseach Charles J. Haughey and me. At that time nobody would have believed that within three short years I would be stepping into Terry's Gucci shoes and becoming the biggest pain in the ass to everyone and anyone inhabiting the social and showbiz classes of Ireland's now famous "Celtic Tiger economy". Keane was, after all, the toast of Ireland's social scene. She was the estranged wife of a judge and the long-term mistress of Charles J. Haughey, the most powerful Taoiseach in Irish history. However, Terry's house of cards would soon come crashing down — and the whole of Ireland would be watching.

TURKEY (JULY 1996)

So how does someone decide to become a gossip columnist? Well, the roller-coaster I was about to get on started as a poolside conversation that same year, when I was just 23 years old. A friend, John McCabe, had invited me to join him and some pals on a two-week package holiday in Turkey. With nothing else to do and nowhere else to go, I managed to get some money together and decided to take up the invitation.

One afternoon John suggested that we visit a friend of his who was staying in another hotel. When we arrived we found the young man and his girlfriend by the pool. During an interesting chat with her she explained to me how she was doing a bit of journalism for *The Irish Times*. I hung on her every word as she told me that her journalism work often took her to screenings of movies before they came out and to launches full of celebrities, and that she even got paid for doing this work. The girl's name was Tara Delaney.

Shortly after our conversation Tara moved into public relations. This is a side of journalism looked down upon by seasoned journalists, or "hacks", as they are known within the trade. According to my college lecturer, public relations was an occupation fit only for failed journalists. Tara was, until recently, Head of PR and Communications for Vodafone Ireland and earning a six-figure salary. So much for my college lecturer's theory, eh?

At this time I was as far away from a six-figure salary as you could get. For some strange reason, I had drifted into working as a bouncer. I think I had become bored with being a waiter and wanted something with a little more excitement. The "excitement" I craved involved me standing at the door of the Dublin bar, Buskers. I was rostered on the afternoon shift for around six weeks until I was let go. Why they got rid of me, they never told me, which was confusing as all I had to do was stand at the door. A few weeks after I had parted company with Buskers, I started work as a bouncer again — this time at the Ambassador Hotel in Kill, just outside Dublin. I was working there before I left for Turkey and when I returned was informed that they no longer had any work for me. I began to suspect that I mightn't be cut out for that particular career.

So there I was — tanned, unemployed and broke. A while earlier I had been living in a flat in Rathgar with my best friend Tony Casey. The only good thing to come from that experience was a meeting with our landlord who happened to be the principal of Ballyfermot Senior College. This College housed one of the best journalism schools in the country, so I applied. I didn't hear anything back — probably due to the fact that I couldn't write, spell or even punctuate very well. On top of that I had only managed five passes in my Leaving Cert. English was certainly not my strong point — a grade C was all I had managed, along with a fail in both Irish and Maths. That was why I never followed my first dream of becoming a hotel manager.

A few weeks later I had forgotten about being rejected by the college. However, in one of those wonderful twists of fate I got a phone call from the college telling me that somebody had dropped out of the journalism course: if I was still interested, the place was mine. I remember the call as if it came yesterday. I was sitting in Milanos restaurant on Dawson Street in Dublin, having lunch with a chef friend of mine called Aidan Chadwick. Aidan had just set up Unique Dining, which has gone on to become one of the biggest outside-catering companies in Ireland. I was working with him as a waiter. The lady on the other end of the phone told me if I had £50 I could join the course the following week. This was the exact moment my life changed forever. At the end of September 1996 the professional waiter Jason O'Callaghan arrived at Ballyfermot Senior College to start a two-year diploma course in Print Media to become a journalist. You have to remember that at that stage in my life I had barely even read a newspaper, never mind written for one.

My only experience with Ireland's paper of record, *The Irish*

Times, was working security there the year before. I arrived into my first class in college and was shocked to find a class of 32 eighteen-year-old students looking back at me. At 23, it felt like I was old enough to be the teacher. The students had just come from doing the Leaving Cert and I had sat the exam six years before. Feeling out of place and slightly stupid, I hid at the back of the class. When asked why I wanted to be a journalist and what type of journalist I wanted to be, I stood up and announced "I want to get free stuff, to go to film premières and nightclubs, to hang out with celebrities and on top of that, to get paid for it." They were shocked at my lack of enthusiasm to oust the evils of society and make the world a better place. They never asked me again.

By late November 1996, I had the first few things I needed for a career as a journalist: "Who? What? Were? When? and Why?" were the basics for any story. Write your "copy" (another journalistic term for your story) so that it can be can be cut from the bottom up, and can fit into the space the sub-editor has for it. And the most important thing — get your facts right. With all that in mind, plus a second-hand 1985 red Nissan Stanza, a cheap word processor and an even cheaper suit, I was ready to take on the power of the Irish media and roll over any stars that got in my way.

Anyone reading this book who wants to be a journalist should remember one thing: the only people who look at and read your byline (the author's name on a newspaper article) are yourself and your mother, a fact explained to us by Darren Hughes, our journalism lecturer in Ballyfermot Senior College. Never was that more true than on the day I got my first byline on December 12, 1996, in *The Echo*.

The Echo was a local paper, read and circulated within the Tallaght region of Dublin. My Page-5 story read "Dealer Cut Drugs Cost" and I think I bought around 10 copies. Des Gibson, a guy who was around my own age and whose whole family were in the newspaper business, was the news editor of *The Echo* at the time. He was the man who published my first story and for the following two months I worked freelance in the paper. I covered the opening of the new UCI cinema in Blanchardstown, where I first experienced the world of celebrity. The actress and singer Patsy Kensit was brought in for the opening. On the same night, I met Tony Tormey, a local actor from the Irish television show *Fair City*. It was Tony who took me to Lillies Bordello nightclub for my very first time. Over the next eight years the Grafton Street venue would become Ireland's top celebrity nightclub and my so-called "office" for gossip seven nights a week.

The Echo was the type of newspaper where young reporters cut their teeth. The guys who showed me the ropes all quickly moved up the ladder of the Irish media after they left *The Echo*. Des Gibson went on to become one of the editors in *The Star*. Michael Clifford became the political reporter for *The Sunday Tribune*, while Myles McEntee joined *The Sun*. David Kennedy was the owner of *The Tallaght Echo* and the first media boss with whom I had a run-in. One day he approached me in the office of *The Echo* and told me in no uncertain terms to get out. That was, of course, after he had realised I had been working on the paper for well over two months, didn't have a job there but was making good use of its facilities. When David fired me, there occurred yet another of those twists of faith.

On the very day I left *The Echo* I got my first story in the national press. *The Star* used my story "Prostitutes in law risk" on Page 23 on January 24, 1997. Dave O'Connell was the news editor and Bernard Phelan the photo editor of the paper at the time. It was the start of a long and fruitful relationship with the paper. The last thing I did before being escorted from the offices of *The Echo* was ring my aunt Anne Chute in France. I explained that I had gone back to college and informed her of my situation with *The Echo*. I needed a friend in the Irish media and I knew my family had contacts with Aengus Fanning, the editor of the *Sunday Independent*. Anne called Aengus and asked him to meet me and point me in the right direction. She was worried about me, as usual. When I had come off the QE2 cruise ship the year before suffering from cabin fever it was at her hotel in the South of France that I recuperated. I had worked on the ship as a waiter for six months and my aunt had always watched out for me ever since my mother died when I was 19.

Things move fast in the world of newspapers and the following day I found myself nervously waiting outside the office door of the editor of the biggest newspaper in Ireland without a clue what I was going to say to him. Aengus Fanning had never met me before, even though both my parents had known him growing up in Tralee, County Kerry. My father had studied in his family home after school, learning from Aengus's father who was my father's maths teacher. My aunt even dated Aengus for few weeks when they were teenagers and my grandmother and his mother were lifelong friends. I can safely say that without that call from my aunt and Aengus's agreeing to see me, my life would be totally different today. At that meeting, Aengus introduced me to Willie Kealy, the paper's news editor. Brushing me off to Willie, Aengus asked did I have any good stories and I babbled out the details of my story on "Drug Dealers Cutting Costs". They went for it. I wasn't going to tell him it had been in *The Echo* two months previously.

That Sunday my first story was published in the *Sunday Independent*. In the space of one week, I had gone from writing for *News at 10*, Ballyfermot Senior College's free sheet, to *The Echo*, *The Star* and the *Sunday Independent* and I was only getting started.

CHAPTER 2

YOU CAN'T WRITE, YOU CAN'T SPELL, YOU'LL GO A LONG WAY

(1997)

With Sir Bob Geldof who would later advise me on marketing ideas for my website company

Globally, the newspaper industry would not be what you would call the most secure employer in the world. So, it was just as well I wasn't pushed on security. After all, at that stage of my life I had no money and no property. My car was worth around £500 and I didn't own anything of any value. Getting a full-time job in the *Sunday Independent* so early in my career was not something I had planned, but none the less I couldn't control my enthusiasm. Which was just as well, because after six years in the paper I still didn't have a permanent job. There was an offer of a one-year contract but I don't think anything was ever signed. I was just a full-time contributor to the paper and therefore self-employed, which meant that I had few rights as an employee. When I became a columnist, I knew that a life of financial "insecurity" was something I would have to become accustomed to. Things like pensions, health insurance and paid holidays were defiantly not going to be part of my life for the foreseeable future.

It was January 1997 and with my first story in the *Sunday*

Independent, Willie Kealy told me something that he probably regretted telling me for the rest of my time at the paper. On the Tuesday after my first story had been printed in the paper I called into the office to see Willie, as he had asked me to do. He casually told me to pop in any Tuesday from then on with any other good story ideas that I had. From that day on I plagued Willie every single Tuesday for six months. Eventually, when I told him of a story about Bono having a party in The Clarence Hotel with David Bowie, he passed me on to Barry Egan.

At this time Terry Keane's diary was written by Terry Keane — well, that was the answer if anyone ever asked. I saw her twice in two years behind the closed doors in Abbey Street, where Independent Newspapers had their offices. Barry Egan was part of a team gathering stories for Anne Harris, the deputy editor of the paper and the brains behind most of the 'Living' section and Terry's column (probably the most read page in the newspaper). I can only guess that before I arrived Terry got tired of writing her column and was then paid a reported £1,000 a week just to let her name be used as the author of the weekly social diary.

This was also around the same time that Gayle Killilea, a friend of Barry Egan's, arrived to work at the office. When I met up with Barry and gave him the Bono/David Bowie story he asked me to write it up as a memo and send it to him. Liam Collins, one of the paper's best reporters and deputy news editor, set me up at a computer and away I went. Over the next few weeks, months and years, I became part of the team that collected stories for Terry's column which over 1.3 million people read every Sunday. Madeleine Keane, who was Terry's daughter, would pop in from time to time to join Barry, Gayle and myself in Anne Harris's office where discussions were held every Tuesday for that week's column. It was a tad odd for me to be in meetings every Tuesday with some of the biggest editors in the country, as I was still in college and hadn't even completed my first-year exams. It seemed as if I was years ahead of everyone else in my class by landing a place in the *Sunday Independent*. It seemed pointless to be sitting in a class learning about becoming a newspaper editor when I could be in an office learning from the newspaper editors themselves.

During mid-1997 I also began work earning £100 a week on the Dublin radio station FM104. My persona on the show was "Jayo from the Paparazzi", and once a week I would go live on air and tell Dublin where the stars were staying, or at least where I thought they were staying, and what mischief they were getting themselves into. A lot of my friends at the time were working as waiters and barmen. The nuggets of information I would get from them would go into Terry Keane's column and then live on radio. During this time I began interviewing celebrities on a regular basis. One of these stars was Sir Bob Geldof.

Originally from Dublin, Geldof had been the front man for the Irish punk band The Boomtown Rats in the late seventies and early eighties. He is, however, best known today for his charity work after he organised Band Aid and Live Aid to raise money for and awareness of those staving in Africa. More recently he put together the "Live 8" charity event which aimed to cancel Third World debt. On the business side of things he has accumulated millions with his website company Deckchair.com and became a highly successful TV producer with his Planet 24 production company which made shows such as the *Big Breakfast* which gave Chris Evans his big break.

Geldof is the type of person who will listen to someone interviewing him and then give the answer he wants to give as opposed to a lot of younger PR-friendly stars who will give you a quote that sounds like it is being read from a press release. He is extremely passionate about everything he does and sees things in their most simple form. He cares very little about fashion. Once, when I complimented him on a nice a jacket he was wearing, he replied with "I don't even know where this came from. Some crowd called Mulberry just sent me over a bunch of suits". His friendship with Bono has come into the public's view more recently; when asked about him Geldof always refers to his friend by his nickname "Bonzo".

Sadly, later that year, with the death of Princess Diana in August and the involvement of photographers on motorbikes chasing her car before the fatal crash, the whole paparazzi thing did not seem as appealing. FM104 and I parted on good terms. Today I still have a good relationship with people like the station's programme director Dave Kelly, the controversial presenters Colm Hayes and Adrian Kennedy, plus the ever charming Margaret Nelson, who is the head of advertising.

A number of friends of mine helped me when I started to break into the Irish newspaper world. My then girlfriend and her twin sister ended up on the front page of the *Evening Herald* due to me. She was then plastered all over the Irish Independent when we took a day-trip to see the QE2 in Dublin. A school friend who looked like George Michael got a full page in the *Evening Herald* in March. A week before, another friend, Stephen O'Donahoe, who was my supervisor on the QE2, got on Page 3 of the *Evening Herald* when he landed a job working as a manager in U2's high-profile hotel, The Clarence.

By June 1997 I was on my summer holidays from college and was back annoying Willie Kealy in the *Sunday Independent*. I had purchased a house and things were going pretty well. One day as I passed his desk he grunted and asked me if I would like to go to Africa. The paper was involved with the charity GOAL, and had assisted the boys' school Blackrock College in their fundraising activities. They needed someone to go to Kenya for 10 days to report on the work GOAL was doing and to write about it for the paper. Everybody else, it seemed, had said no to the trip. I felt obliged as I was the last port of call for Willie. Planning for the trip began with me being sent for my jabs to protect me against every type of disease. A month later I flew to Nairobi.

Now please remember that I was a guy from Walkinstown in

Dublin, whose primary education had been in Crumlin and who had attended secondary school in the tough inner city's CBS Synge Street — a total contrast to Blackrock College. I was spending my nights trawling Dublin's nightclubs looking for gossip. To find myself suddenly in the middle of Nairobi was a culture shock, to say the least. For the first few days we spent our time visiting the shocking slums of Nairobi after meeting up with Irish nuns based near the area. We visited shanty towns held up by wood and corrugated iron and saw children who spent their days in disease-infected water collecting empty plastic bottles to sell. To see what these people endured on a daily basis and to notice how happy they still were was truly inspiring as much as it was saddening.

A few days later, we left Nairobi and drove for seven hours. Much of my time was spent in the back of a pick-up truck as I watched Africa go by. Driving through tiny villages it was amazing to see that some of the inhabitants kept zebras in their gardens as pets. As we crossed the equator we saw flocks of pink pelicans on the great lakes. We visited Nairobi National Park and watched the elephants and giraffes in their natural habitat, which was a real thrill.

We travelled late into the night and ended up in the Rift Valley, 500 miles from Nairobi. Our driver was a priest from Inchicore in Dublin. He and two other priests had gone to Africa to breed camels for the poor Pokot tribes of the region. The whole set up seemed very "Indiana Jones" to me, and the one thing that always sticks in my mind was how the priest handed me a torch and a stick when I was going to bed. He told me that the torch was to see where I was going so I could make my way to my hut in the dark and the stick was just in case I came across any snakes. I didn't have to use the stick on any snakes but did have to use it when I got to my hut and found a huge scorpion in the sink. During my few days in the Rift Valley, I got to meet some of the world-famous Masai warriors, whose only worldly belongings are a spear and a small oddly shaped piece of wood they use to sit on.

Ironically, MBT trainers (the MBT stands for Masai Barefoot

Technology) are now on the market and aim to rid the stars of their dreaded cellulite. You have to wonder how much the warriors are due to receive in royalties.

During this time I also got to experience the taste of all types of dodgy animals and visit the natives in their mud huts. Coming from a materialistic society and with the dawning of a new millennium, it was strange to imagine people living on little or no income and spending their nights in mud huts which they shared with their entire families and even some of their animals. There were without television, electricity, mobile phones, supermarkets and even running water. Yet they seemed happy as long as they had the basics of food and shelter, unlike a lot of the many spoilt rich stars I have come across.

A few weeks later I was back in Ireland and down in Tralee, County Kerry, the place where I was born. My family had moved to Dublin when I was a year old and I had not been back to Tralee for five years since I had buried my mother. My visit this time was to meet Neil Armstrong, the first man to walk on the moon. There wasn't much time to sit and chat with him as he was bustled in and out again leaving the press little time to see him, never mind chat to him. To me he seemed like a man who turned up, signed autographs and made a living out of having been lucky enough to get out of the spaceship ahead of Buzz Aldrin, who will forever be known as the second man on the moon. Even though I had spent most summers growing up in Tralee, I had few relations left, and being there without my mother for the first time was a lot to handle.

When I got back to Dublin I was offered the chance to fly a Mig fighter jet. The plane had been used in the James Bond movie *Goldeneye*, and the promoters, Smirnoff Vodka, had brought it in for a media promotion. My flying experience lasted around 10 minutes before nausea got the better of me. It wasn't very James Bond, but it had been an amazing experience all the same. To hear the pilot's call sign of 'Mig' was a lot different to hearing the air hostess on Aer Lingus announcing the drinks trolley. The heat inside the cockpit of a fighter jet is stifling, and to go up above the clouds within seconds is something I will remember for a long time, nausea or no nausea.

By September 1997 I was auditioning for the job of waiter yet again, but this time for an article in the *Sunday Independent* about Irish citizens looking for a £4-an-hour job working in the soon-to-be-opened Planet Hollywood restaurant. Towards the end of the year I ended up writing a lot of small pieces for "The Keane Edge". One of the stories concerned Robbie Williams dining in the Grill Room of the Berkeley Court Hotel before doing a concert in the Olympia Theatre. He was so unfashionable with the public then that nobody even noticed him in the restaurant. His show in the venue had an audience of just over 1,000 people and there was no good scandal from his visit because he was just not newsworthy at that time. He was sorting out his weight issues as well as his well-documented drink and drugs problems. He only had one or two singles which had barely made a dint in the charts by that stage in his career. Then 'Angels' came out and he went into orbit overnight. Back then no one would ever have guessed that years later he would play to 6,000 people at The Point theatre and over 80,000 fans at the Phoenix Park, becoming one of the biggest solo artists in the world. Someone once told me in confidence that Robbie had asked them to manage him and they had said no, having felt that Gary Barlow was the one from Take That who would be the star. Oops.

At around the same time I did one of my first stories on Michael Flatley, who had just split up with his wife Beata. Flatley is one of those guys who loves the sound of his own name and completely believes in his own celebrity. He's an extremely self-confident guy, but I guess that self-confidence like that comes with having €500 million in the bank. Being self-made this guy knows how to party and knows how to share his good fortune with everyone around him. Thankfully for us, Flatley is always up for a laugh with the press and the photographers.

In November I discovered that the then President of Ireland Mary Robinson was using the same hair stylist as The Spice Girls, which is always a useful item for a gossip columnist. This interesting information came from a hairdresser who was working for a top Irish company that took care of the President for all her State business. It just happened that The Spice Girls were in town that week doing a video and this company got the call and ended up styling the video shoot for the girls. It's a pity that the girls didn't ask the President to take a cameo role in the video.

I ended the year going back to college, trying in vain to look interested enough to finish the year with a least a pass in my Christmas exams. During 1997 I had travelled around Africa, completed one full year in college, managed to avoid getting arrested for driving my £200 motorbike (the car had died) without tax, become part of the biggest newspaper diary team in the country, and started and ended a radio slot. Looking back it had been a good 12 months, and I knew that 1998 was going to be even better if I was wiling to stick my neck out far enough.

Now sticking my neck out was something I had become an expert at doing since I was very young. During 1992, while working in Paris for the opening of Disneyland, I persuaded a French friend who worked in the uniform section of the resort to give me a security guard's uniform. I told him that U2 were coming to the opening of the theme park and I had to translate as they spoke only Irish. He actually believed me and I spent a few days before the opening getting in everywhere, including all the VIP opening parties, dressed as a security guard. The highlight was when I met up with the American group The Four Tops. After telling them that I was their appointed guide for the duration of their stay, we had a ball partying with the stars for the opening weekend. I did get caught off-guard when they brought me on stage on opening night to sing the song 'My Girl' with them and The Temptations. To top it off, the event was broadcast on world television. Thankfully, nobody in charge spotted me.

The following day, while I chatted to Levi, the lead singer with the Four Tops, outside the New York Hotel, the actor Eddie Murphy, who was an invited guest for the opening, strolled by to say hello to him. I was star-struck but afterwards Levi gave me some of the best celebrity advice anyone has ever given me. He said, in his gruff American accent, "Boy, I've met everyone from presidents to pop stars — hell I knew Michael Jackson ever since he was a little boy — and the one thing you got to remember about celebrities is that they all drop their trousers and piss the same way." Worldly advice and something I will remember for years to come.

Three years later, when I worked on the world-famous QE2 cruise ship, I nearly stuck my neck out too far. We were travelling from New York to Southampton and I was on hand-baggage duty with a friend of mine from Scotland. Hand-baggage duty meant we had to get dressed up in our white uniforms, complete with white gloves, meet passengers once they arrived at the ship, and then take them to their cabins. One day as we walked back down to the gangway in New York, I saw this stunning blonde struggling with two children and her bags, so I rushed to the rescue. As I started churning out my Irish charm, I spotted a man arriving onto the ship behind her. The blonde's name was Rachel Hunter and the man was her husband, Rod Stewart. He chatted to my friend about Scottish football of which Rod is a massive fan. I chatted briefly with Rachel as she carried one of her kids and pulled the second one behind her by the hand. I always remember the kids — each had a small tattoo on their leg, even though they were only around three or four years old.

CHAPTER 3

THE BOYZONE AND SPICE GIRL YEARS

(JANUARY–JUNE 1998)

The next big thing. Take That's Gary Barlow, yours truly and Boyzone's Ronan Keating

I was once told that my skills as a journalist would land me the editorship of a red-top tabloid by the time I got to my mid-30s. The funny thing is that the person who told me that was Anne Harris, the deputy editor of the *Sunday Independent*. At the start of 1998, I went back to college with my first newspaper column as proof that I was making progress. During the Christmas period I had hung around the Sindo (newspaper jargon for the *Sunday Independent*) and got my first break. Djinn Gallagher was a sub-editor who had joined the paper from the *Sunday Tribune* and was editing the Terry Keane column. In early January Djinn was asked to stand in and do her own diary while Terry's had a break. I got to do a small showbiz column under hers on the back page of the paper. According to my cuttings, the date was January 4, 1998, and the headline read 'Hot Limos and a dash of Spice'. Reading it now shows just how star-studded Dublin was at the time. The column mentioned The Spice Girls holding court in the K Club in Kildare (another place where I once worked as a waiter). Temple Bar was full to the brim with stars like Willem Dafoe, who was filming with the Oscar-winner Mira Sorvino, ex-girlfriend of the French actor Olivier Martinez, who is currently dating the singer Kylie Minogue. Mira was staying in Dublin with her boyfriend, director Quentin Tarantino. At the same time Kim Bassinger and her husband Alec Baldwin were staying in the Shelbourne Hotel with their daughter, Ireland.

U2 were hosting Christmas parties in their hotel and a young chef called Conrad Gallagher was making waves by opening his second restaurant and poaching five staff members from The Clarence Hotel restaurant. He was to become Ireland's first celebrity chef; we would be hearing a lot more from Conrad over the next few years. Michael Flatley was staying in the Westbury Hotel and was partying after picking up a national entertainment award. Rockers Joe Elliot and Rick Savage from the band Def Leppard were in the newly refurbished Lillies Bordello nightclub, with those hairstyles that time forgot.

By March I was back on Terry's diary and covering the launch of Ireland's first men's magazine, aptly titled *Himself*. It didn't last. Uma Thurman was in Ireland for her honeymoon with her new husband, actor Ethan Hawke. Their first baby was due in July but she didn't let that get in the way of her retail therapy in Dublin. I spent the day chasing her around Dublin's biggest and most expensive department store, Brown Thomas. The couple were very much in love at that stage and he was a much bigger star then she was back then. She bought clothes and cosmetics and he just wandered behind her like so many men in departments stores around the world.

Also during March a selection of world-famous stars hit Dublin for the première of *The Man in the Iron Mask*. Sadly, the movie's biggest star, Leonardo DiCaprio, failed to make the trip. However,

Gabriel Byrne, John Malkovich and Jeremy Irons made up for the missing Titanic star. Byrne gave me a detailed interview about DiCaprio and how he felt that the young star would be the next big thing. He felt DiCaprio wanted to fly below radar — just like Johnny Depp, a heartthrob who wanted to turn down pretty-boy roles and be known more for his acting than his looks. Years later you can see how Byrne was right, as DiCaprio got nominated for an Oscar for his portrayal of Howard Hughes in The Aviator.

Gabriel Byrne is one of those actors who is known as an "actor's actor": he loves to act and is not really too interested in the fame or the money. (Although I heard he recently bought a villa in the South of France, so the money isn't hurting him too much.) Byrne is very calm and takes being famous as a silly side effect of his job. I once met him in the Horseshoe Bar in Dublin's Shelbourne Hotel, where he was sitting in the corner reading *The Irish Times*. He said hello and then went back to his pint of Guinness and his paper. Something that only happens in Ireland. Can you imagine that happening in LA or London?

In April 1998 I landed my first full-page interview in the Sindo. Anne Harris told me that it was my big chance. I wrote over 1,000 words after a long interview with Jason Barry. You have to remember that 1998 was the year of the multi-Oscar-winning movie Titanic, which launched the careers of Leonardo DiCaprio and Kate Winslet. Jason Barry was from Artane in Dublin, and was chosen by the film's director James Cameron as Tommy Ryan, DiCaprio's very Irish friend in the movie.

My interview was good, but obviously not good enough, as I never got to write a full-page interview again. It may also have been due to the fact that I was cheeky enough to do a similar interview with him for the *Sunday World* and Anne was, understandably, far from impressed. In the interview, Barry talked about his friendship with DiCaprio and how they had attended the Oscars together the year before. After the awards, they attended the famed *Vanity Fair* party. Two months earlier I had met Barry at a Planet Hollywood

Oscars party in Dublin, where we both enjoyed an interesting night with the actor Jean Claude Van Damme. It was the same night that Titanic swept the boards at the Oscars. DiCaprio was at the Oscars and Barry was in Planet Hollywood with me. Shows you how close the duo were, doesn't it?

DiCaprio is now one of the world's leading actors and Barry is still trying to make it. He can be seen these days in a series of ads for Guinness. Barry did talk to me about DiCaprio, saying he was a very down-to-earth type of guy and just one of the boys on the set. DiCaprio's influence on Barry was only overshadowed by the real star of the movie, which was the ship itself. James Cameron had built an exact replica of the liner in Mexico and Barry told me how jaw-dropping it was to go over the hill next to the set and see this massive ship just sitting there. "When I first set eyes upon Titanic I guess I felt the same way her passengers did back in 1912. It was amazing." Barry told me. He also explained how the actor Matthew McConaughey, was the first choice for the lead role in the movie and it was only after he had turned it down that DiCaprio got it.

Myself with Jean Claude Van Damme and Jason Barry at the Planet Holywood Oscar's Party

As I already mentioned another guest at the party was the actor Jean Claude Van Damme. When the actress Michelle Collins, who had recently left the hit BBC soap opera 'EastEnders', arrived at the party Jean Claude's eyes lit up. Van Damme, who was famed for his drug issues was, let's just say, in a "tired and emotional" state. He wanted to meet Michelle but was too lazy to walk over to her. Instead, as I was sitting beside him at the time, he asked me to invite her over. Wanting to oblige and sensing the possibility of a good story I wandered over to the back of her chair and whispered in her ear that Jean Claude Van Damme wanted to have a drink with her. Before she got a chance to answer, a voice came from her far side. It was her boyfriend, who told me to tell Jean Claude that if he wanted to have a drink with Michelle he could join them. He declined. But I got to write the whole thing up for *The Mirror*, with whom I had started to work.

I was still writing for Terry Keane's column but was also working full time with *The Mirror*, while also being in college full time. I was chasing stories about the relationship between Ronan Keating and his new girlfriend, model Yvonne Connolly. There was a story going around that Ronan had been dating one of Yvonne's model friends before hooking up with her. Then, literally overnight, Yvonne and Ronan got married. The funny thing was that the story of their secret wedding was a bigger shock for Ronan's manager Louis Walsh than for anyone else. Ronan and his wife-to-be had gone on holiday to the Caribbean island of Nevis and tied the knot. I was in *The Mirror's* office at the time when the news leaked out that the couple had wed with only Ronan's brother in attendance.

We were genuinely shocked and could not believe it. Within minutes I was on the phone to Louis Walsh. He was also in a state of total shock, even more so than we were. Boyzone and Ronan were Louis's big break. He had been around the music industry for 20 years making a not-too-good living on the back of small-time bands. In 1993, with £5,000 from his business partner John Reynolds, Walsh formed Boyzone as an Irish Take That, and now his sexy lead singer had married in secret and was about to break the hearts of every record-buying teenage girl. Louis need not have worried, as Ronan would go on to become a very successful solo artist and Louis's new band, Westlife, were about to become the biggest boy band in Irish history.

In time Louis would end up becoming bigger than most of his acts. I remember when I started writing stories in the papers getting phone calls from Louis constantly plugging his bands on a daily basis. Now you would find it hard to get him on the phone as his fame gets bigger and bigger with shows such as 'The X Factor'. The thing about Louis is how hot and cold he blows. One day you would meet him and he would rip you apart for no reason; the next he would give you an all-access pass and buy you a drink. For a while he was hated by the press. He had Ronan Keating, Samantha Mumba and Westlife on the go and some thought he got very big for his boots. His old friends in Dublin and some journalists who had known him a long time were getting pissed off at his attitude. I remember Bryan McFadden demanding I be taken backstage at a Westlife concert and Louis saying no. Then he let in two of his friends from *The Sun* and *The Star*. A while later he got me backstage at the MTV awards in Sweden and even took me there in the back of his chauffeur-driven car. That's Louis Walsh for you.

SUNDAY People

65p

FREE DIANA SOUVENIRS JUST FOR YOU

BOYZONE TO SPLIT AS RONAN GOES SOLO

The Sunday People, breaking the hearts of all the little girls

At around the same time the American model Caprice was in Dublin and was hanging around U2's hotel. Victoria Smurfit was getting her big break in the new TV show 'Ballykissangel' and Bono was making rambling speeches at the *Hot Press* awards in Belfast. On May 10, 1998, I wrote my first Page 1 story for *The Sunday People* newspaper. It was one of many Page 1 stories I would write over the years. The headline read 'Boyzone to split as Ronan goes solo'. The story came from a security guard working in the shop where Keith Duffy's wife worked at the time. I did the story about how Ronan was planning to leave the band after Boyzone's next world tour. It was the beginning of the end for Ireland's biggest pop band.

Shortly after this, Louis Walsh recommended me for a full-time job in *The Mirror* as temporary replacement for Ritchie Taylor. Well, at least that's what Louis was telling everyone. Ritchie was their showbiz reporter and was leaving to join *The Sun*. I made more money in eight weeks in *The Mirror* than I had in six months in the *Sunday Independent*. *The Irish Mirror* had the budget of a UK tabloid and wanted stories on the stars. They weren't interested in socialites like those the *Sunday Independent* had me chasing. They wanted scandal and they wanted as much of it as I could get.

I had, however, at this stage got my own column in the *Irish Independent's* 'City Living' supplement. This supplement came out every Tuesday. I had heard that the reporter writing their diary had left and I asked around the Indo about who the editor was. They sent me to talk to a man called John Spain, the features editor. I found him at his desk in Abbey Street and an hour later I had my own column in the *Irish Independent* with Myles McWeeney, a well-seasoned Indo diarist. 'Out on the town with Jason O'Callaghan' was my first weekly column. Not bad, I thought, as I was still working for the *Sunday Independent* and *The Irish Mirror*, and, let's not forget, I was also coming towards the end of my second year in college with final exams pending in June.

The *Irish Independent* diary got me known, but most of the events were far from exciting. The first diary was about the battle between Lillies Bordello and Renards, two of Dublin nightclubs catering for the elite of the capital's social scene. Names on the circuit during the first week of May were mostly those who had recently been on Pat Kenny's television show. These included Mandy Smith, the former model and then girlfriend of Rolling Stone Bill Wyman, Kevin Kennedy (Curly from the TV soap *Coronation Street*) and Julian Lennon, son of John. Lorraine Keane was also floating around at the time and working in AA Roadwatch as an announcer.

Bob Geldof was also back in Dublin and talking about setting up a 24-hour music radio station in Ireland called Atomic Radio; sadly, it never took off. Names like the Carter Twins popped up in my column regularly back then, as did that of the singer Kerri Ann. Both were involved with Louis Walsh and both of them are long forgotten, proving the point that Louis Walsh may have had the Midas touch with Boyzone and Westlife but a lot of his acts never took off.

In May Yvonne Connolly made her first outing as the new Mrs Keating and did her last job as a model. Every paper in Ireland turned up at the photo-call and Nokia, who had booked Yvonne before the wedding, couldn't believe their luck. When Ronan and Yvonne made their first public appearance together as a married couple, what passed between the newlyweds and I is the stuff of tabloid legend. I want to mention before I tell this story that what ensued lead to us becoming enemies for over five years. This is the first time the truth about why we fell out has been written. Thankfully, Ronan and I are friends today and have worked together over the past few years. Back in 1998 and 1999 things were very different. So different, in fact, that after he got married in the middle of 1998 he chased a photographer working for me down a road while shouting abuse at him.

The whole fiasco started one day when I got a call that Ronan and his wife were shopping in Brown Thomas for items for their new home. Having arrived I was subsequently followed around the store by security — not because they were worried I was going to steal anything, but because they knew who I was and what I was doing in the store. Once I had caught a glimpse of Ronan and his wife, I left to wait outside. A few minutes later I spotted them walking out the back of the store towards the Powerscourt Centre. Now bear in mind this was the first time they had been spotted together in Ireland as man and wife and it would have been a good pic to get. So I sent over a young photographer who was working with me at the time to ask politely if he could take their photo. Ronan got very upset with the snapper, said no way and started shouting at him. I have no idea why he was so irate at the snapper but he was.

I decided that we would sit it out and wait for them to leave the shops. A few minutes later we spotted them entering the Royal College of Surgeons car park nearby. We went outside and waited for them to drive by. The young photographer had chickened out by this stage and I knew if Ronan saw me he would go nuts.

As luck would have it I bumped into an old school friend of mine called Tony Talbot who took the photographer's camera and waited at the ramp at the exit of the car park. Ronan's car came out and the singer immediately slammed on the brakes, got out of the car and chased Tony down the road. I turned my back so that Ronan could not see my face as the two of them flew by me with Ronan screaming. Tony outran him, but to this day I wish Ronan had caught him, just to see what he would have done. Later, I made a call and got reports all over the radio about Ronan being abusive to one photographer and chasing a second one. The story was great but I made no money because even after everything that happened we had no pictures and the radio stations don't pay for stories. It took me another four years to become friends with Ronan and his wife again. Looking back it had been very funny to watch.

June's diary was full of stories about bands such as Dove (which included Hazel Kaneswaran, later to become a star of the TV show Popstars – 'The Rivals' and a judge on 'You're A Star') and the girl band FAB (whose members included Tara Lynch, the younger sister of Shane from Boyzone). A new IMAX cinema opened in Dublin with a big VIP attendance, only to close a few short years later. Comedian Patrick Kielty turned up to the Budweiser Irish Derby with his new girlfriend, model Amanda Byram. Who would have thought that today he would be left in the shadows while she is making a huge name for herself in America. In July I wrote how The Edge from U2 had to use his father as a connection to get on the membership list for the Royal Dublin Golf Club. Luke Goss of the eighties boy band Bros was in Dublin's The Point theatre making his debut in the hit musical Grease. It was supposed to be his showbiz comeback but all he's done in the years since was appear on the reality TV show, 'Hell's Kitchen'.

One day I had to leave *The Mirror* early. When asked by the news editor why I had to leave I had to admit that it was to sit my finals in college that afternoon. When he asked what I was studying, I had to further admit that it was journalism — the job he was paying me a full-time wage to do. During my time at *The Mirror*, I had worked under the great John "Jumbo" Kearns and Neil Leslie (now the managing editor of the *Sunday World*). Both of them taught me a great deal about tabloid newspapers, like to use the words "spine chilling" frequently.

During my time with the paper I interviewed Tate Donovan, now the star of the hit television show The 'OC' and the ex-boyfriend of Jennifer Aniston. He was a dull as dishwater, in my opinion, and seemed to have the IQ of a table lamp. Jennifer had just dumped him for Brad Pitt. Tate rattled off the standard line which most famous guys or girls will give if they are single and doing press interviews in a certain country. If it's a famous female star she will say how she finds Irish men very sexy, or Swedish men or Russian men, once it applies to the country she is doing the press interview in at that time. The famous actor or male singer will insinuate that he is looking for a nice Irish girl or French girl, etc. You get my drift. The paper will then run the headline 'Jennifer's ex is looking for an Irish girl'. The star gets his publicity and we get our story.

Shortly afterwards my stint in *The Mirror* came to an end as the paper got its new showbiz reporter from the UK. His name was Neil Michael and he had ended up breaking the story on Sinead O'Connor becoming a priest. It just so happens that he was also dating her at the time. His career was short-lived in Ireland, as was their relationship. Sinead is an interesting person. I've heard that if she doesn't like something that has been written about her in a paper, she will burst into the newspaper's office and lay into the hack that has written the article. She hates paparazzi photographers even more and thinks that they are total scum who make a living off other people. We shared some time over the years and at one point we even lived in the same apartment complex. I've always found her very deep and interesting but I would also see a manipulative side of her as she is a very smart girl but as hard as steel. Not someone you would cross.

On June 8th a story landed in my lap from a friend who worked in a video shop. A garda friend of his had told him that the son of one of Ireland's biggest cabaret singers, Dickie Rock, had been arrested. Ritchie Rock was picked up by the Gardaí with a friend who was carrying over £3,000 of uncut heroin. Dickie's eldest son Jason was a good friend of mine and I made a call to him telling him of the story. Dickie Rock rang me and explained that his son was just in the wrong place at the wrong time — and that's how the front-page story in *The Mirror* read. The story ran for days in the press and was covered on all the radio stations. It just shows how beneficial it can be for a personality like Dickie to use the press to get their side of the story across, unlike the hordes of clueless stars who turn against the press and then wonder why the press have turned against them.

'BROODY' POSH KEEPS MUM OVER STARTING A FAMILY

WRITE ON: Two youngsters were delighted to get Posh Spice Victoria Adams' autograph when she went shopping with her sister Louise PICS COLIN KEEGAN

BABY SPICE?

EXCLUSIVE

By JASON O'CALLAGHAN

POSH SPICE had babies on her mind when she went shopping in Dublin city centre yesterday.

Broody

The Irish Mirror exclusive that nearly made my carrer

A few days later I was talking to a security guard I knew at the Westbury Mall in Dublin. After 20 minutes of idle chatting he mentioned in passing that Sporty Spice, Melanie C, had just gone into the gym behind the hotel. Now bear in mind this was the week after Geri Halliwell had left the band and the world was looking for the rest of The Spice Girls. This guy had just found one and it was only now he decided to tell me. Within seconds I was in the gym posing as a new member and having a good look around. I saw her and then went outside to make a few phone calls — to every paper in Ireland. This was also the day I also figured out why they call her Sporty Spice, as it was over three hours later when she left the gym. As she walked out the door I had sold the story to everyone — newspapers, radio, magazines. I wrote the words and got the photos for both the *Irish Independent* and *The Star*, as well as selling the information to all the other papers for a fee. We even got some great shots of her buying underwear in Marks & Spencer which I got onto Page 1 and Page 3 of both the papers I was working for that day.

However, it was only a few days later on June 12 that I missed what might have been the biggest scoop of my career with a young woman called Victoria Adams, a.k.a. Posh Spice. She would later become Victoria Beckham, wife of the footballer David Beckham and the most photographed woman in the world after Princess Diana.

I had heard she was shopping with her sister on Grafton Street in Dublin. I saw her buying baby clothes but she refused to make any comment on whether or not she was pregnant. A few weeks later she told the world that she was expecting the couple's first child, and, understandably I was gutted. I had been the only journalist to talk to her and get photographs of her buying baby clothes. If she had told me first about the baby I could have retired that very day. Like most celebrities I would meet and work with, telling the truth was not one of their strong points.

CHAPTER 4

WHO THE HELL IS COLIN FARRELL?

(JULY–DECEMBER 1998)

With Colin Farrell at the launch of th Dublin Film Festival.
No matter who you are you will look like shit in a photo with him.
Pic.: Gerry McDonald

In the *Sunday Independent* I was working closely with Barry Egan who was over me in a supervisory role. I had also become close to Trevor Danker who was an old-school type of reporter. He had once had dinner with one of my heroes — Frank Sinatra — so it was an honour to work with him. Trevor did a male version of Terry's social diary except he was still actually writing his own column. He took early retirement from the Sindo not too long after I arrived but his advice about the social circuit was invaluable to me when I was starting off and I thank him to this day.

I had just left *The Mirror* and had finished my exams. I was still doing my pieces for the Terry's column for around £150 a week, which I suppose was a bonus as I had started off at £50 a week. *Ireland on Sunday* was a small Sunday paper that had developed from *The Title*, a Sunday sports paper. The man running the show was Liam Hayes, a former Meath footballer and the editor of the paper, which was now launching a lifestyle magazine. I was out of college a few weeks and hadn't even got my results when they offered me the job of editor of the magazine after two interviews. I was going to take it, but in my heart I knew that, despite their faith in me, I was no way qualified to run a magazine at that stage of my career. I politely turned them down and used the contract from the paper to get myself a pay rise in the *Sunday Independent*.

So I was now out of college and ready to work full time on Terry's column, making my first outings at some of Dublin's high-profile social events as an official gossip columnist. One of my trade secrets at the start of my career — and the only reason I started to get into these events — was that I noticed that Terry Keane was never in the office. Furthermore, piles of invitations were gathering dust in her post box. All the PR companies thought she was writing the column. As I was getting no help from anyone in the paper, I just started opening the invitations and attending the events myself, telling the organisers that I was her representative and that she was at another event and had sent me along in her place. This was as close to the truth as I could get. Anne Harris once summoned me to her office and said that someone had told her I was parading around Dublin as Terry Keane. I told her that a 25-year-old young man and a fifty-something lady could in no way be confused. It was not Anne Harris's fault; I suppose she was just doing her job. There were many nasty little people I would come across who would lie to get themselves in with powerful people in the newspaper business like Anne.

A few years later I remember being asked by Anne if I had been drunk outside a club in Dublin and demanding to be let in after being abusive to the staff. I think it was only then that she found out that I was a teetotaller and didn't even smoke, never mind drink alcohol. Anne never asked me anything like that again. In the end it was discovered that some guy was pretending to be me to benefit from a few freebies. There was video footage from a security camera of him claiming to be me and I was cleared. Silly things like that were always happening in the world of newspapers and editors have to trust their reporters. It takes time to build that relationship so when you are new at the game they don't trust you.

In August 1998 Lorraine Keane went from working as the voice of AA Roadwatch to becoming TV3's entertainment correspondent and a public figure. Lorraine was a typical Celtic Cub; she was also one of the first people that I feel the *Sunday Independent* made into a celebrity. She would talk about her private life to us and pose for photographs without hesitation and was very good at playing the media game. We would meet up and chat about her engagement to her then boyfriend. It was all just part of the business, which she was smart enough to understand.

During the summer, Pierce Brosnan, the James Bond star and Navan-born actor, was back in Ireland. He was filming a production with Irish Dreamtime, his new company. The movie was called *The Nephew* and it was produced by Brosnan and a woman called Beau St Clair. At the time she was in a relationship with the film's main star, Donal McCann, who played Brosnan's nemesis in the movie. Sadly, McCann died of cancer a while later. I was the one who told Pierce Brosnan about the death of his friend and co-star: I had called his publicist in LA, Dick Guttman, on the day it was reported in *The Irish Times* that McCann had died. Dick asked me to fax him the article, which he passed onto Brosnan from me. I had also made contact with the actress Angelica Huston, whose father, the famed director John Huston, had directed McCann and Angelica in the film *The Dead* some years earlier. Huston's office sent me an email with her tribute to McCann but it was Brosnan who was totally shocked at the news. So shocked in fact that at 7am the next morning my mobile rang. It was Brosnan on the other end.

Now as you can imagine, it's not every day you get a call from James Bond. So, in my half-awake state I tried in vain to make some sense of the words coming out of my mouth as Pierce Brosnan told me how upset he was by the death of McCann, whom he described as a Knight of Ireland. He was shocked at the news and continued by saying what a fine actor McCann was and that he hoped in time to become half as good an actor as him. I did not want to be cruel-hearted, but I have to admit I was equally interested in getting a scoop while I had one of the biggest actors in the world on the phone. I asked Brosnan where he was ringing me from and he said Bora Bora in the South Seas, where he was on holiday. I was in my house in the working-class suburb of Clondalkin in West Dublin. Our lives were so far apart that I said goodbye and went back to bed depressed.

Brosnan is one of a select number of stars who tries to give something back to the country in which he was born. He ensures that every fourth or fifth film he makes is made in Ireland, despite knowing that they are not going to be blockbusters, so people around the world can see just how beautiful Ireland is. He himself left the town of Navan when he was just seven years old to move to the UK with his mother after his parents separated. She remarried and Brosnan only met his father, Tom Brosnan, once again before he died.

Speaking of the meeting Brosnan said "I just opened the door one day and there he was. His first words to me were 'You're a fine looking fella'. We had a chat and a drink and then he left. A while later he died." Recently I told Brosnan that I often thought about his father when I visit my own mother's grave in Tralee in County Kerry as the graveyard is full of people with the name Brosnan. He just said "Tom and a lot of his family were from Kerry so it's wouldn't surprise me if he was there, but I'm not sure where he is buried."

On September 1, I wrote in the *Irish Independent* about a day I spent with Louis Walsh and Shane Lynch from Boyzone. Louis and I sat in the Thunder Road Café in Temple Bar while Shane signed autographs. Louis told me of a problem he had with his new boy band. They were called IOU and Louis asked me what I thought of the name "Westside". Louis, together with the band's record boss Simon Cowell, had agreed on the name, but within days had found out the name was already taken by a rap band in the USA.

Simon changed the band's name to Westlife and within a year they had their first Number 1 single 'Flying without Wings'. The rest, as they say, is history. By 2004, they had the amazingly achieved close to the same amount of Number 1 singles as The Beatles.

I had first met them (Westlife, not The Beatles) in 1999 and had found them to be very nice, quiet guys, shy and new to the scene. If I was asked to describe them after knowing them for six years I would say I get on best with Nicky and Shane. Once I did a half-decent version of 'Mack the Knife' outside Lillies Bordello nightclub in Dublin with Kian. Mark is very publicity-shy and is very quiet in person. A total gentleman, he refuses to act like a spoilt pop star and is, I'm told, planning a career as a producer after the band retires. I would give them another year and predict that they will have gone their separate ways by the end of 2006. But who knows? No one thought they would last this long.

On Fitzwilliam Square later that month, Dublin came to a standstill for the arrival of the U2 express. U2 are the world's biggest rock band as well as Ireland's biggest export, so when they took over the plush streets of the square to film their new video for the song 'The Sweetest Thing', I just had to be there. The video was a homage to Bono's wife Ali to make up for his forgetting her birthday one year. Everyone from Boyzone to Riverdance were drafted in for the video shoot. The video had Bono being carted along the street in a horse and carriage as he tried to make it up to his wife with over-the-top gestures. Sadly, we in the press were not invited to take part in the shoot but we had another wonderfully exciting day standing around being bored for eight or nine hours.

By October, The Spice Girls were back in town and recording their third album in the Windmill Lane Studios in Dublin. U2 were reported to be in the studio next to them, but God only knows if that was true. It was also the same month that the late great Chris Roche, one of Ireland's top PR men, put on one hell of a party for the Dublin première of *The Phantom of the Opera*. It was a party that to this day has not been equalled in the capital. It had everything a good party needed, starting with an endless budget. I always think that if you are going to do something then do it right. Spend the money and don't be a cheapskate. This party had some of the best food and plenty for everyone, and, more importantly, a constant flow of free drink. There were different rooms with different music, each one decorated for the style of the party using props from the show. No burly security staff and access to everyone in every part of the event. In other words, no roped-off areas for certain VIPs. Just a great night out and a pleasure to be a part of.

In November, I found myself interviewing the film critic Barry Norman, who had just left the BBC to host a TV show on Sky television. After 26 years at the BBC Norman thought that moving to Sky was the right thing to do. How wrong he was —the show was axed and he hasn't been heard of since.

On the week of November 25, I saw something that should have given me a clue of things to come. At an art exhibition in the Origin Gallery (where I also met Mick Jagger and his wife, the model Jerry Hall) on Harcourt Street, I spotted my boss. Well, in some respects she was my boss. It was Terry Keane in the flesh, chatting to the great Charles J. Haughey, the former and now-disgraced Taoiseach. One of the worst-kept secrets in the media and one of the biggest in Irish politics was about to raise its ugly head on live television not too long afterwards.

In December the cracks that I had talked about months before which would lead to Boyzone splitting up were starting to show. The band were desperate to break into the US before they broke up and Louis Walsh was telling white lies in order to keep them in the press. Some of these lies I unwittingly printed in *The Star* newspaper were about the band signing a $10million-dollar deal in the US. Of course they hadn't signed any deal but when a band's manager tells you these things you just have to listen.

Then suddenly none of that mattered, as it was at that time that Ireland's biggest movie star since Pierce Brosnan was about to be discovered. Towards the end of 1998, the actor Kevin Spacey came to Dublin to make a low-budget movie called *Ordinary Decent Criminal.* The film has long since been forgotten, but the story goes that before filming, Spacey spotted a young actor while at a play in London. The young actor ended up with his first major film role in the movie, and the word is that it was thanks to Spacey. A short while after filming, Spacey told a film director friend about the Dublin actor and the director, Joel Schumacher, auditioned him in London for a new movie. The actor was the last one of 44 young men reading for the lead part in a low-budget movie called *Tigerland.* The young actor's name was Colin Farrell.

An exlusive photo of Colin Farrell aged 14 in Castleknock College where he was a model pupil. His tough hardman image is something he created when he made his way into moves to gain credibility

Farrell had started his working life in Dublin as a waiter, just like me. He worked in the Elephant and Castle restaurant in Temple Bar and then as a country-and-western line-dancer in a venue called Break for the Border. Thankfully, I never followed him down the line-dancing route. He had made the move into acting with a small role in the BBC television series 'Ballykissangel'. From the upper-class suburb of Castleknock in Dublin, Farrell had started out in the Gaiety School of acting with funding from his older brother Eamon, who ran a dance school. He had left the school once he got the role in 'Ballykissangel'. Over the next three years, Farrell's career would rocket, but while he was making movies, few were big in Ireland until late 2002.

I once met Farrell in the UCI multiplex cinema in Dublin. He was with his mother and sister after leaving a movie. Not one of the hundreds of moviegoers even noticed him. He had just been to see the film *The Others* staring Nicole Kidman, which was cute, as he had just finished filming *Minority Report* with her ex-husband Tom Cruise. It was a Sunday night and the day the *Sunday World* had just broken the story of Farrell's split from Amelia Warner, whom he had married three months before. We caught each other's eye, and I could see his sister telling him who I was. However, we just said hello and I left him alone. It was a golden opportunity, but we were both off duty and he was just on a night out with his family. If he had wanted to talk to me he could have. Today, he can't walk five feet without getting mobbed. I remember in 2000 trying to get the *Sunday Independent* to write about him and I was shot down and told that he wasn't even known. I guess things have changed since then.

Oscar winner Kevin Spacey, the man who really discovered Colin Farrell. Pic.: John Dardis

By November 1998 I was in Milan, attending my very first MTV music awards. The amount of bullshit surrounding these awards shows is enough to drive you crazy. If you are in the press, you need to get accreditation to get into certain events like the MTV awards. However, if you are in the Irish press you get nothing but hassle. Coming from a country that has produced U2, Sinead O'Connor, the Corrs, the Boomtown Rats, Thin Lizzy, the Cranberries, Van Morrison and Enya, to name but a few, you would think we in the Irish press had a right to get into major music awards ceremonies and cover the events for our population of four million people? No, being from an small island nation you get treated like a leper.

Dolores O'Riordan from The Cranberries. Despite having some of biggest bands, Irish press are still put at the bottom of the list for global media events. Pic.: John Dardis

I eventually got the accreditation I needed to get into the awards after selling my soul to some PR girl from MTV. Once I got into the awards I was pushed into a back room with one or two hundred other journalists from around the world. Just when things could not get any worse my luck changed. Few of the journalists spoke English as most were South American, Russian, Eastern European, French, German or Italian. Thankfully, the few of us who could speak English got to ask the questions to the majority of English-speaking celebrities who came into the press room. With me in the press room was Ruth Scott from 2FM radio and my nemesis Paul Martin, a new and young showbiz reporter who had joined *The Mirror*. He will forever be known as Ireland's second best showbiz reporter and that's the burden he has to carry. Paul was one of the few people who was in attendance with a tape recorder and who recorded the famous incident of my Madonna interview in Milan. This was the interview during which the material girl took the piss out of my accent in front of the world press.

In the press room word went around that she was going to come in and do some interviews. The buzz was electric when she entered the room surrounded by burly bodyguards and some of the Italian police. In a stroke of luck yet again I was next to the MTV guy who had the microphone when it was time to ask the questions. I will always remember being handed the microphone and seconds later having an out-of-body experience as I heard myself saying "Hello, Madonna". I asked her about the rumours that she was buying a new home in the UK and if she had ever visited Ireland.

During her answer she admitted she hadn't been to Ireland but would love to go and then continued our conversation by taking the piss out of my Dublin accent, to the amusement of my journalistic peers. She started with "Haven't you a funny accent?" but in the midst of her fun stopped to give me some razor-sharp answers to my questions about her buying a new home in the UK. "No, I haven't bought a house yet in England. I have just been looking," she stressed to me. I found her intimidating and she came across as someone who had been dealing with tabloid reporters for years and was not about to misquoted by me or by anyone in the press. For weeks Paul played the interview on his radio slot in Northern Ireland and I guess I will be forever known as the 'Man Madonna Took The Piss Out Of'.

At the end of November one of the very first stories appeared about Celia Larkin, the then girlfriend of the Taoiseach, Bertie Ahern. He had come to power a year before. We all knew he was separated from his wife, but now we had to deal with his new girlfriend. Celia was spotted around this time shopping in Dublin with Cherie Blair, while her husband Tony, the British Prime Minister, was dealing with Government business with Celia's boyfriend, Bertie. It was after this time with England's first lady that Celia earned her nickname as "the first girlfriend" in the press.

CHAPTER 5

HELLO MR WILLIS

(JANUARY–JUNE 1999)

With Bruce Willis, who is overjoyed to meet me. Pic.: John Dardis

At the start of 1999 I was becoming known around the media circuit in Ireland as a paparazzo journalist. I didn't take this as an insult because the truth was that I was one. I wasn't a paparazzo journalist by choice. It was more to do with the fact that I had to be a media mercenary to get stories for the papers. Good showbiz news is the fodder of the tabloids and they were the people paying. *The Irish Times* was definitely not interested in my type of journalism.

In January I found myself in County Wicklow running around trying to establish the facts behind a story on U2's manager Paul McGuinness. News had surfaced that he had been involved in a car accident. McGuinness, the fifth member of the band, as he is known, was the man famed for making U2 the band they became. However, just before Christmas he was nearly a manager no more after his Jaguar crashed into a jeep near his home in Annamoe in County Wicklow. Thankfully he was okay, but it wouldn't be the last time McGuinness had a run-in with someone. The next time, however, it would be with me.

By the end of the month, I was gatecrashing again. This time it was a concert by Robbie Williams, who was about to kick off his world tour in The Point theatre in Dublin. This was only a year after he had barely sold out the much-smaller Olympia Theatre. Robbie had barred the press from his opening show and once I got in I could see why. The singer had an entire screen full of tabloid cuttings about his ups and downs on display and it seemed to be his way of hitting back at the press.

Over the next few years Robbie and I would come into contact only once, in the dressing-rooms of Brown Thomas when he was getting ready for a date with the Irish singer Andrea Corr.

Now at this stage let me openly admit that I made two bad journalistic mistakes in 1999. The first was to do with Robbie Williams. It concerned a story that he had ordered footballs to play with during rehearsals in The Point and that he had ordered more footballs to play with while staying at the plush, five-star Merrion Hotel. The story caused huge hassle and it was only after it was published that I realised I had been stitched up by someone trying to get publicity. The story about the Merrion Hotel appeared on the front page of *The Star* and Robbie went mad when he saw it. To Robbie Williams, I apologise.

Shortly after that I was back on course and broke the story that Ireland was set to host the MTV Music Awards for the first time.

By February, I was still writing pieces for Terry Keane's column in the Sindo but that was soon to change as a dark and scandalous cloud was rising on the horizon. It was one that would leave the whole country, including me, in shock. Terry Keane was secretly planning her final days in the paper and her big exit from public life was to take place on the same night as Gay Byrne would host his second-last 'Late Late Show' after nearly 40 years.

During this time I was spending my days checking the listings magazines and finding out what stars were flying in to do concerts and what hotels they were staying in. As they arrived I would get their photo and sell the news of their arrival to the papers. Each week we would find out who would be guests on the talk shows, and then we'd hang around outside RTÉ and follow them out on the town. Using this method, I ended up with a Page 1 in *The Star* on February 11, 1999. The British actor Peter Bowles, star of the hit TV show 'The Irish RM', missed a night's sleep due to the antics of the Manchester United footballer Dwight Yorke in the Westbury Hotel. Bowles had been lined up to do a number of interviews the following day, but due to his lack of sleep he failed to make any of them and Dwight's partying in the next room was the reason.

By February 14 I had covered the opening by Bono of Perry Ogden's photographic show in the Hugh Lane Gallery. Then we had the arrival of Hollywood stars Kim Bassinger and Alec Baldwin, who were back in Dublin again and enjoying St Valentine's night in Conrad Gallagher's Peacock Alley restaurant. During this time I also wrote the very first words about a young man who today is expected to be as big as, or bigger than, Robbie Williams. In the *Irish Independent* in early 1999, I covered the Entertainment Awards in the National Concert Hall, an event that has since become the Meteor Awards and is now held in The Point theatre. At the awards were bands such as East 17, 911 and B*witched, now all long gone and forgotten. At the awards a young singer called Bryan McFadden, who was with Louis Walsh's new band Westlife, caught my eye. At the time I thought he had an amazing resemblance to the actor Leonardo DiCaprio and I mentioned it in the paper. To this day he still remembers that compliment. Even when his marriage to Kerry Katona was falling apart and he was leaving Westlife for a solo career he still gave me his first interview thanks to that comment.

Later that month at the première of a low-budget movie called *Southpaw* I first met someone who would do great things with his career thanks to genuine talent; his name was Brendan Gleeson. A former schoolteacher, Gleeson has since starred in every type of Hollywood movie from *Mission Impossible 2* with Tom Cruise to *Troy* with Brad Pitt. It's amazing what six years can do to your career if you are genuinely talented.

With a true actor, star of Gangs of New York and Cold Mountain, Brendan Gleeson at the Irish Film ball during the days he was stil doing theatre

Les Misérables was about to open in The Point theatre. After the success of *Phantom of the Opera*, "Les Mis" had already taken in over £3 million in pre-show sales before its opening night. This was also around this time I got the Page 1 story in *The Star* about how Bono had undergone an operation on his throat. The story came from a cleaner I knew who worked in the exclusive Blackrock Clinic. Bono's wife confirmed the story to me and said that the operation was a success and that her husband was due to make a full recovery. At this time in my career I was finishing up my diary with the *Irish Independent*, working for a number of tabloids and still doing Terry's column with the team in the Sindo.

By March I wrote about an intimate dinner Hollywood star Kurt Russell and his partner Goldie Hawn had had with her daughter Kate Hudson in the Fitzwilliam Hotel in Dublin. Kate was in Ireland filming a low-budget movie called *All About Adam*. Her co-star was a young unknown Irish actor called Stuart Townsend, the current boyfriend of the Oscar-winning actress Charlize Theron.

Now I had a feeling at this stage that April was gearing up to be a wild month: Robbie Williams was in town chasing Andrea Corr; Bruce Willis was coming to Dublin to party. I wanted to be at the centre of both events. So, on Friday, March 26, Hollywood wild man Bruce Willis flew into Dublin. The story of Willis's visit to Dublin started in Joxer Daly's pub on the north inner city. No one raised an eyebrow at the arrival of two men at the end of the bar in the middle of the afternoon. It was only later that someone mentioned that the man in the woolly hat had been Bruce Willis. He had asked his chauffeur to take him somewhere on his way from the airport where he could have a pint of Guinness in a real Irish pub. His driver Mick Devine had taken him to Joxer's. After his Guinness, Willis made his way to Planet Hollywood on St Stephen's Green to greet over 1,000 VIP guests. At that stage, the restaurant chain had over 40 premises all over the world that were owned by stars such as Willis, Sylvester Stallone, Arnold Schwarzenegger and Bruce's ex-wife Demi Moore.

The night started with Bruce taking to the stage with a host of Irish stars such as Mary Black, and being watched by Ronan Keating and an array of world-class snooker players who were in town for the Irish Open at Goffs. Willis ripped the place apart, playing with his own band, The Accelerators, until around 1am. Then the actor and singer, who was well into his forties, took to the decks as DJ for the rest of the night. By 3am, Bruce was still going strong, and as the crowd dwindled Willis showed no sign of slowing down. By 6am, only around 60 people remained as he started to dance on tables and drink Jack Daniels like it was water. I reported on the event for the *Irish Independent*, the *Sunday Independent* and *The Star*, plus a number of radio stations. But it was what happened at

7am when Willis was about to leave the party that made things a lot more interesting. Willis had spotted a dark-haired waitress called Sheila Ryan at the party, and after going wild for seven hours he invited her back to his hotel, The Merrion. He had flirted with the young girl after she had dropped a tray of glasses and he had come to help her pick them up. Sadly, by the time Shelia made it down to the hotel in one of Willis's cars, the actor's bodyguards stopped her going up to see the star. The reason is one we will never know, and one I'm sure remains to this day a secret between Willis and his bodyguards. All I know is that I wrote the story up after meeting Ms Ryan and then getting Page 1 in *The Star.* The nice thing was that Bruce's chauffeur dropped Ms Ryan home from the hotel.

IRISH WAITRESS WHO CAUGHT THE EYE OF

Bruce spent the night flirting then invited Sheila back to his hotel...

LOOKS FAMILIAR: Demi's old hairstyle is so like Sheila's

PARTY TIME: Hunky Bruce singing during recent trip to Dublin

EXCLUSIVE
By JASON O'CALLAGHAN

THIS is the stunning Irish waitress who became a leading lady for Hollywood star Bruce Willis during his recent trip to Dublin.

Performed

Recovering

The Star tells everyone of Bruce Willis wild night out

There was good news for Ronan Keating and his wife as their first child was born in Dublin. I got to spend the night hanging around outside the hospital freezing my ass off, trying to spot any stars coming in to see the new baby. Nobody came and I got a cold.

By April 7 Andrea Corr was denying claims in the UK press that she was dating the manager of The Spice Girls, Simon Fuller. We quoted Andrea but she very rarely talked to us. Instead, we would mostly talk to her via her business manager who would give us the quotes. Over the next few days, the Irish press were lead around by the nose as reports surfaced that Andrea was set to hook up with Robbie Williams. The proof of Robbie and Andrea's relationship came when the couple were spotted hugging in Renards nightclub. They then arranged a date for the following day. First thing the following morning, both Robbie and Andrea were spotted in Brown Thomas shopping for new outfits for their date that night. That was the day I went looking for Robbie and walked straight into him as I left the dressing-room in the store. Everyone in the press was trying to find out where and when the date was. However, instead of hitting one of the capital's fancy restaurants or exclusive clubs, the couple were taken up the Dublin mountains to Ireland's highest licensed premises, Johnny Fox's pub, for dinner. It took a few hours for us to discover the location, and the only guy who found them was a photographer called Colin Keegan, whose niece just happened to be drinking in the bar at the time.

That was how most of us found out where and when things were going on. Friends, neighbours, staff — anybody who knew you would give you a call if someone famous was around. The relationship and the date did not work out. Corr was said not to be interested in Williams and the couple failed to see each other after that. They both tried to say it was just a meeting about a duet but the idea of two artists meeting without managers and agents is just silly. So, it was the end of the romance between two of the biggest stars of the time.

At the end of April I wrote a highly embarrassing story about the massive Irish girl band of the time band, B*witched, who by then had four Number 1 singles under their belts. I revealed that Sinead O'Carroll from the band was not 19, as her record company was claiming. In fact, she was six years older, turning 25 the next month. I knew she was older because I got a copy of her birth certificate from the office of Births, Marriages and Deaths. The information I needed to get the certificate came from a girl I knew down the country where Sinead had applied for a job and left her CV before she joined the band. A few weeks later I exposed the other two girls in the band, twin sisters of Shane from Boyzone, who were also telling lies about their age. It may not change the world, but it was a good story at the time and was the talking point of all the radio shows for the entire week.

Louis Walsh was defending himself in the press against Shane Lynch's mother after saying in a *Sunday Times* interview that Shane, Keith and Mikey from Boyzone were just passengers, and that Ronan and Stephen had all the talent.

Now, I mentioned earlier that I made two big mistakes in journalism, both of which took place in 1999. The first was the football thing with Robbie Williams and the second involved the actress Martine McCutcheon from EastEnders. She had been in town with Sony, her record label, to appear on Dave Fanning's Sunday morning television show. I had copied some of her interview and wrote a story about her being in Dublin and staying in the Herbert Park Hotel. My story appeared in *The Star* and the *Irish Independent* and my mistake was to say that she had spoken to me when I should have said she had been speaking to Dave Fanning. A publicist from her record company wrote a letter to the *Irish Independent* saying that I hadn't had an interview with her and that my quotes had been taken from the television show. Looking back at the scalding I received from the news editor of the *Irish Independent*, I still don't see her point as this type of thing is common place in the media world.

Anyway, today I sing with my own show and frequently sell

out concerts. Like most artists I would not care about where my quotes appeared once they were right. I had given her a write-up in the biggest daily paper in the country and due to the fact that they would not give me an interview I robbed some quotes from a television interview to make the story. Was it really so bad? It was the last time I would do that and the last time I would take any shit from a publicist.

Also at this time, the *Sunday Independent* was fawning all over Conrad Gallagher. Nobody seemed to care that he was just a chef but our gossip column was filled to the brim with news of his love-life. Yes, the love-life of a chef from Donegal was the topic of the day. Looking back, I am more confused than anyone else as to why we were writing about his split from his partner, Domini Kemp. She was the last person who wanted to end up on the back page of the paper. Back then, he was only getting started on the lady front but this subject of Conrad's love-life would fill hundreds of column inches over the next few years. I personally think we made Conrad a celebrity in the paper by writing about him every week and Conrad then started to believe in his own stardom.

Even though she turned me down for coffee, myself and Andrea Corr eventually made up

Andrea Corr was at the top of my wish-list again by May, as she was enjoying life to the fullest with a new man. This time it was Huey Morgan, the lead singer of a New York band called The Fun Lovin' Criminals. Huey even dedicated a song to Corr at his Belfast concert. By the end of the month it was over, and Andrea was spotted out to dinner with another mystery man. At this stage, even we gave up trying to keep up with her.

The diary in the *Sunday Independent* during May looked and felt the same as any others we had done over the previous two years. It featured stories about the love lives of comedian Patrick Kielty and the then TV3 presenter Amanda Byram. It contained mentions of upcoming social and fashion events and a number of mentions about the 'Late Late Show' and its guests, which included such names as Joan Collins.

Few were to know what was coming on the second-last 'Late Late Show' and how it would change my life.

CHAPTER 6

GOODBYE TERRY, HELLO POSH

(JULY–AUGUST 1999)

Police and press gather outside the Irish Castle where Dave Beckham and Victoria Adams marry

There was so much happening throughout the summer of 1999 that I will have to dedicate a whole chapter just to cover this eight-week period alone. At the start of July, I was chasing the finer details of Posh Spice and David Beckham's wedding. It was to be the first of a string of massive showbiz weddings in Ireland, as at that time our little island nation seemed to be extremely fashionable with the celeb set.

So with the upcoming wedding taking up so much of my time it was surprising that I found myself in front of the television watching Gay Byrne's second last 'Late Late Show' one Friday evening. I was too tired to head out to RTÉ, where the show was being broadcast, so I just went home and chatted to my father, who was watching the show. Gay's star guest that night was Terry Keane. She sat down and then proceeded to tell the entire country that she had been the mistress of Charles J. Haughey, the former Taoiseach, for the past 20 years. She went onto admit that she no longer wrote her column in the *Sunday Independent* and that she had left the paper that very day. Terry said she had given the paper her notice and was going to work for *The Sunday Times*, the *Sunday Independent's* main rival.

John Ryan, a young man who shortly afterwards started *VIP* magazine — an Irish version of *Hello!* — was then the editor of the culture section of *The Sunday Times*. He, like me, had earned his stripes in the halls of the *Sunday Independent* and he was now stealing its greatest asset. A short note on a blue piece of paper had been given to the *Sunday Independent's* editor on the day Terry went on the 'Late Late Show', explaining her plans. She wrote the story of her long-term affair with Charles J. Haughey over the next few weeks in *The Sunday Times* for a record fee and sales went through the roof.

I just remember sitting at home in shock and waiting for my name to be mentioned. She never said my name, but did tell the country that other people had been ghost-writing her column for the past number of years. The big question for the editors of the Sindo was: what would they do now? I was kept out of the loop and was too busy anyway with the Posh Spice wedding to worry about what was to become of the back page of the *Sunday Independent*.

Now I had met The Spice Girls a few times. The first time was when I ran — literally — into Geri Halliwell in Brown Thomas after I heard she was shopping in the store. I was in such a rush at the time that I ran right into her and nearly knocked her off her feet. The next time I met a Spice Girl was when David Beckham and Victoria were dating and they were in Dublin having dinner in Planet Hollywood. While I waited outside they escaped out the back door, but we still got their photograph. That's something that always puzzles me about celebrities: why do people want to become famous and then wear dark sunglasses so that no one will recognise them? Running out the back door of a restaurant is silly. If you are a smart star you get a nice posed photo as you leave a restaurant. If you are dumb (as they were) you get your photo taken beside some dustbins as you run out a back door into a dirty laneway.

The big wedding was to take place in Luttrellstown Castle near Lucan on the outskirts of Dublin. A week before the event we wrote the story that Beckham's ex-girlfriend, who was then dating his Manchester United team-mate Gary Neville, would be attending the wedding. Posh wasn't too happy with that. A day or two before the wedding, which was planned for July 4, we got a scare. The Beckhams were spotted in a castle in Scotland and rumours began flying that the wedding would be moved there. Thankfully, it was only for a photo shoot, and the following day the bride and groom arrived in Ireland for what was being called the "Irish Royal Wedding".

On Saturday, July 3, the private jets started to arrive as the cavalcade of stars descended on Dublin for the weekend. Manchester United footballers and Spice Girls were popping up all over the place. George Michael and Elton John were to play at the reception and, notably, Geri Halliwell was off the guest list.

So on the sunny summer's day that was July 4, 1999, I found myself outside the gates of Luttrellstown Castle awaiting the wedding of the year. We had all thought about trying to get into the wedding, but only one photographer, Tony Kelly, who worked for *News of the World*, beat the security and got into the castle. On the day before the big event, he managed to get a selection of shots of the massive King- and Queen-style thrones the couple were to sit on as they received their guests.

To the theme music of Disney's *Beauty and the Beast*, the couple walked down the aisle in the mid-afternoon sun. Swans and geese had been brought in to roam around the grounds along with 70 security guards flown in from the UK. The security guards were there to protect *OK!* magazine's million-pound investment in the wedding, which was then the highest paid to any couple for a wedding. Victoria had the word "obey" taken from her vows in honour of The Spice Girls' image of Girl Power. The couple asked for no gifts but for donations to be made to a meningitis charity.

Over 375 guests enjoyed the party dressed in black and white outfits, the colours Victoria had asked her guests to wear. Nearly 400 people were working inside the castle on the wedding and outside 150 members of the world's press were hanging around the castle walls also working. To this day, I still get calls when the footage of the wedding is shown on TV as it shows me running across the front of the coaches as they arrived at the wedding with a big smile on my face.

With the wedding over it was time to send in the invoices to the tabloids and head back over to the *Sunday Independent* where they were scrambling to find someone or something to replace Terry Keane. I can't tell you what happened behind closed doors as I was never trusted enough to be let in on the big secrets. I do know they asked everyone who was anyone in the social whirl in Dublin at the time to replace Terry.

'The Keane Edge' column disappeared from the end of May 1999. But the column was to continue under the comical title 'Not the Keane Edge' without missing even one week. This was to prove to the column's million-plus readers, plus *The Sunday Times*, and the *Sunday Independent's* critics, that even if Terry was no longer a part of the column, it would still live on. With Terry out of the way and her reported salary of £50,000 a year back in the paper's budget, the editors now wanted to prove the team could do a better job than ever. It was also time to go to war with the Sindo's former golden boy John Ryan, who had so publicly embarrassed the paper.

It was never officially said on record but if you look at the column for June, July and August 1999 you can read for yourself how many times we attacked and made fun of both Terry and John. The attacks began on May 30, but the real fight was to start a week later on June 9, at the launch of John Ryan's new *VIP* magazine. The question around Dublin was why someone would buy *VIP* magazine to read a feature with some "B–rate" Irish star, when they could buy *Hello!* or *OK!* magazines with real celebrities on the cover for the same price. By 2005, *VIP* was the biggest-selling magazine in the country after the *RTÉ Guide*. What this says about Ireland's social elite and the Celtic Tiger, I don't know. The fact that the *RTÉ Guide* is the biggest-selling magazine in Ireland is the thing that worries me.

Dodgy photos of John Ryan started appearing in the column, and tales of how Terry was going on radio shows saying she regretted selling shots of herself and the former Taoiseach to *The Sunday Times* were common. We did, of course still find time to write about those completely unimportant people that I will forever hate writing about. Such as Karla Elliot (an ex-wife of an ex-rock star), Olivia Tracey (an ex-Miss Ireland), and Patricia Devine (a model), all, of course, friends of the editors. We covered the launch party of John Ryan's new magazine *VIP* and ripped the piss out of it beyond remorse.

News-wise, the diary's team still came up with the goods about stars and their habits. We wrote of Michael Flatley's search for an Irish home — in the end he picked Castle Hyde House in Cork. We also started finding new people to make fun of each week. Celia Larkin, the girlfriend of the Taoiseach, was our number-one target. Celia worked for the Taoiseach in Government Buildings before their affair became public. She bought a nice house in Castleknock in Dublin at around the same time for £250,000, which we wrote about. Soon after that, she left her job in the Government to become a beauty consultant.

The ongoing fight with Terry Keane and John Ryan continued into June, when I even contacted *Hello!* magazine to see if they were going to sue VIP for stealing their format. *Hello!* didn't care about *VIP*, even if we did, even if we were running out of ideas on how to take the piss out of Terry and John. By the start of July the *Sunday Independent* was still looking for a replacement for Terry and 'Not the Keane Edge'.

Liam Neeson, the only star I have ever seen press photographers ask to have their photos taken with

We continued churning out the stories as they discussed what to do with the diary. We wrote about Van Morrison and Michelle Rocha and how in love they were; how Celia Larkin was not allowed to attend the funeral of Cardinal Hume, as she was not Bertie's wife. We wrote about stars such as Daniel Day-Lewis and Jim Sheridan attending a concert by Marianne Faithful in Vicar Street; Liam Neeson being in Dublin for the première of his new movie, *Star Wars*. We hit nightclubs with Jade Jagger, Mick's daughter, and wrote more crap about Michael Flatley's love-life. Plus our regular brown-nose pieces about those who were friends of the diary, but virtually unknown to anyone who did not live in Dublin 4: model Patricia Devine and her attempts to become an actress; plus, Lorraine Keane and Conrad Gallagher, whom we just kept on writing about nearly every week.

We did get stories about famous people on occasion, like the Donegal actress Roma Downey, who landed the lead role in the TV show 'Touched by an Angel'. She had just divorced her husband and these days she is dating a man called Mark Burnett. Burnett is the multimillion-dollar man behind shows like 'Survivor' and 'The Apprentice' with Donald Trump.

We also wrote stories about semi-famous people for whom, it would seem, being famous was just too complicated. These were people such as the TV presenter Liz Bonnin. There was a time when Liz hosted the RTÉ kids TV show 'The Den'. She moved up to the fashion show 'Off the Rails' a few years later. From my experience, Liz is one of those people who want to be famous but then don't want to be written about. I tried in my time as a gossip columnist and a tabloid reporter to get well-known names to play the game, because at that level that's what it is — one big game. Ask anyone from Pierce Brosnan to U2, who are totally professional and know how to play the press. Do a photo, give a quote and you'll get very little bad press.

By the end of August 'Not the Keane Edge' was coming to an end. The last diary we did broke the story of Jim Corr and his new girlfriend, the former Miss Ireland, Andrea Roche, finally coming out as a couple. We showed Eddie Irvine and his new girlfriend Anouk Voorveld being photographed together for the first time, and wrote a story about Terry and Anita Coleman, who had bought Ireland's most expensive house at Number 1, Sorrento Terrace. Shortly before that I had mistakenly written a story that the actor Jack Nicholson had bought the house. It wouldn't have been so bad if the *Sunday Independent* hadn't run with the story on the front page. To make matters worse, the famed US tabloid *The National Enquirer* picked up the story and ran it all over the world. In the end, Jack Nicholson had to deny the story himself. I hid under a rock for a week or two and when I came out from under it, somehow the *Sunday Independent* was about to make me an offer I couldn't refuse. My own column.

CHAPTER 7

THE BIRTH OF 'THE DOUBLE EDGE'
(SEPTEMBER–DECEMBER 1999)

The edited version of the cover of In Dublin magazine giving me my new title of Dublin's Most Dangerous

On August 15, 1999 Gayle Killilea and I wrote our first column in the *Sunday Independent*. Anne Harris had asked us to write our own separate diary each week for the back page and I was honoured. Taking over the helm of a column written for years by Terry and read by a quarter of the population of the country was a daunting task for me but I was up for the challenge. I remember Anne expressing how unhappy she was giving the diary to journalists who were so young — not because we weren't good enough to write it, but because of the pressure she knew it would put on us.

Our first two diaries were split into two on the same page. It was only then that Anne came up with the name 'The Double Edge', following in the tradition of 'The Keane Edge', with our initials at the end of each story we had written.

Gayle and myself on the masthead of the Sunday Independent *when we were revealed as the new face of the social diary*

Our first few diaries consisted of parties in Marbella, premières of shows like *Jesus Christ Superstar*, stories on new boy bands, the love-lives of politicians and the escapades of visiting celebrities. Added to this mix was our ongoing battle with John Ryan and his new magazine *VIP*. Plus concerts, pregnant television presenters, fashion shows, nightclub openings and Irish rock gods such as Bono and what they were up to on a weekly basis. We had our own list of favourite targets, about whom we were expected to write about nearly every week.

We started friendships with some of Ireland's most powerful families which made great fodder for the page, especially the relationships of their rich spoilt kids. These were the so-called Celtic Cubs. They were attending every party and every rich boy had a top Irish model on his arm.

Bono's wife was having babies. RTÉ's Anne Doyle had a new boyfriend. Actor John Hurt had moved to Ireland and had started to date an Irishwoman called Sarah Owens. Ronan Keating got the call-up to host the first ever Irish MTV awards in Dublin. A date with Andrea Corr was being auctioned off at the Barretstown ball for charity. Michael Flatley was hitting the town with a new woman called Lisa Murphy on his arm. I knew Lisa from my teenage years when she used to go to a club run by Valerie Roe, who later took over the running of Lillies. Lisa dated one of the bouncers in the club and over the years, before she met Flatley, I would see her every now and again around town. The story goes that she couldn't get into Lillies one night and as she was turning to leave met Flatley who was on his way in with Dave Egan, the then owner of the club. Flatley took an immediate shine to her and the rest, as they say, is history.

In the paper we (patronisingly) called her the "Tallaght Temptress", named after where we believed her family home was located and her amazingly short skirts. Years later we found out she was from Ballinteer in Dublin and not Tallaght after all. Ballinteer was far more middle class than the working class Tallaght.

Flatley is not like most stars who long to keep their private lives... well, private. Michael Flatley always seems to do the opposite. Once both *The Sun* newspaper and I were called to send a photographer to wait outside Conrad Gallagher's Peacock Alley restaurant on St Stephen's Green to get a shot of Lisa and Flatley. Due to the short notice of the call, both photographers were late arriving and the couple had left to see a show in the Vicar Street music venue. When hearing that both photographers had missed the shot at the restaurant, Flatley, via his publicist yet again, paid for a taxi to drive the two boys up to Vicar Street where they got the shots for the next day's paper.

By October 1999, the charity ball season was in full swing. The Angel's Quest ball, the Sinatra ball and the Tiger Trust ball were all being covered by our new *Sunday Independent* 'Double Edge' column. My ongoing relationship with Pierce Brosnan's office was going from strength to strength, with a good exclusive at least once a month from Dick Guttman, Brosnan's publicist. He was keeping me abreast of news from Brosnan regarding his girlfriend Keely Shaye Smith and their plans to marry. In the end, the wedding would be two years later in Ireland, and I would manage to break in.

Next up for the diary was the Tourism Awards and the Carton ball, which we had to cover and both of which were about as exciting as staring down a toilet bowl. Now, that's the thing about having what most people think of as a "cool job". Yes, you get paid to go to black tie balls, parties, premières, hang out with stars and get everything for free. Yet it is sometimes very boring and it is always hard to get good stories. The hardest thing for some social and showbiz reporters to realise is that while we write about the stars we are not stars ourselves, so it is impossible to compete with them by trying to have the same quality of life that they have. When you are attending these events every night you have to get to know a whole table of strangers, talk shite, get a story, keep the organiser happy and stay sober — not to easy when everyone else is getting pissed and having fun. That's the job and you have to have the discipline if you want to be successful as a social diarist.

In Ireland we have very few real stars, but at the top of the VIP list for any event is Bono. Bono only graces a small handful of events in Ireland each year. Normally, the events he will attend are for his friends, like the artist Guggi, when he opens a show, or Gavin Friday, when he starts a new play. But I'll get back to Bono later.

At the opening of Guggi's new show with the actor Woody Harrelson. You can just see Bono in the background. Pic.: Mark Doyle

By November the pages of the diary were being filled with people on the social circuit like Cathy Reynolds, the daughter of the former Taoiseach Albert Reynolds, who was at the helm of Ireland's first Louis Vuitton shop in Brown Thomas. I guess this was the official start of Ireland's new image as a trendy cosmopolitan city. During the mid-Nineties we had come from an island of pints of Guinness and stay-at-home mothers, to a café society, with women taking some of the most powerful jobs in the country and everybody scrambling to get on the property ladder.

It was the most exciting time to be the face of a social column, as during Terry Keane's years few new restaurants and bars were opening as the country was in a recession. However, during the late nineties, people like John Reynolds were opening ultra-trendy clubs like the POD, celebrity chef Conrad Gallagher had a chain of very trendy restaurants, and a string of hotels like The Four Seasons, The Morrison, The Merrion and The Fitzwilliam were all taking over from older hotspots such as The Shelbourne and The Berkeley Court. Each week our post baskets in the *Sunday Independent* would be full of invitations to new bars, restaurants and hotels. It was time for the beautiful people to come out and show off what they had.

Irish people in general had always hidden their money as if they should have been ashamed of it and ashamed of being successful. Now, with magazines such as *VIP*, they could attend events and show off their Gucci handbags to the masses. It was vulgar, but the new Celtic Cubs didn't care. They were getting jobs in the media and public relations. They were watching 'Sex and the City' and driving BMWs while living in newly built apartments in Malahide. They were eating in new restaurants built, it seemed, just for them — restaurants like Bang on Merrion Row and Shanahan's on St Stephen's Green. They were drinking in the new super pubs on Dawson Street and afterwards heading to Lillies and Renards, the two nightclubs of choice for the beautiful people.

What was happening outside the circuit was of no interest to us in 'The Double Edge'. We didn't look down on those outside our circuit — I couldn't anyway, as I was one of them — but the idea was to give the illusion of a golden circle that everyone wanted to be a part of. If you were not going to the places we were writing about you just were not really on the scene in Ireland, and for some that was like wearing last season's Jimmy Choo shoes. A sin of the highest order.

As for us, we were right in the middle of the glamour and we loved it. We covered the races, and hung out with the O'Reilly's and the Dunnes. We attended balls with Government ministers, sometimes even with Bertie Ahern himself. And more was to come. The final sign that Ireland had changed for the better came in November when the good and great of the world came to attend the MTV awards in The Point. Names like Alicia Silverstone and Kenneth Branagh started to appear in our diary each week as the awards came closer. Spice Girls were being spotted all over town (yet again) and royalty such as Sarah Ferguson, the Duchess of York were popping up in Cork, where she hosted a secret fortieth birthday party.

Then, out of the blue on November 7, it was clear that all our stories on Bertie Ahern's love-life had ruffled some feathers. We had reported that Celia Larkin, his girlfriend, was hoping to work from her home but had not applied for the planning permission needed to change a residential property into one used for business. Then to piss her off even more I invaded her fortieth birthday party in the Westbury Hotel. I had really done everything I could to stir things up a little and then one night in the K Club things took a new direction. It was there at an art sale (why I ended up there, I have no idea, but I did) that I was first introduced to a lovely soft-spoken lady called Miriam Ahern. It was only afterwards that it clicked with me that this lady was the official first lady of Ireland and the ex-wife of the Taoiseach.

At this stage, Bertie Ahern had been in power for two years. He was parading around Catholic Ireland with a girlfriend on his arm for all to see. At that time the general public had not seen his wife in newspapers or magazines. I'm sure, like me, most thought she must be some terrible witch with some serious issues if she had just disappeared into the mists of history once she had separated from Bertie. Otherwise, why had none of us ever heard of her or seen her?

Miriam was a classy, stunning lady and very charming to chat to. Unlike Celia, who would never talk to us and always ran away if she saw us coming, Miriam was someone who we could talk to and write about week-in week-out. Over the years I would become close friends with her, and from what I could see she had spent the last few years taking care of her two daughters. Once the younger daughter, Cecelia, was 18, she decided it was time for her to make her comeback into society, a society she had last graced 10 years earlier when Bertie was Lord Mayor of Dublin and they were still together.

Miriam was, however, put to the back on my mind as later that week came the night I had been waiting for my entire career: the MTV Awards which were for the first time being held in Ireland.

For the first time a decent awards ceremony in my own backyard, and the UK press would have to grovel for once.

The city was going wild with the presence of stars such as Britney Spears, Christina Aguilera, Mariah Carey, Whitney Houston, Mick Jagger, Bono, The Corrs, Pierce Brosnan, Geri Halliwell and Marilyn Manson. I enjoyed the actual night of the awards from the press room backstage, and got to everyone, including the likes of Puff Daddy. After the awards were over, every star was having a party. Whitney Houston and Mariah Carey headed to the Temple Theatre for an R&B party, while some of Puff Daddy's crew got into a row with Shane Lynch from Boyzone.

The highlight of the night was the Iggy Pop party in the Hot Press Hall of Fame on Abbey Street, which has since been renamed Spirit. When I say to this day that I have never seen as many stars in one place as I did that night, people don't believe me. While Iggy Pop was on stage, Bono climbed over the balcony and swung down the ropes over the stage, standing on speakers to get onto the stage with Iggy. Then Bono, Iggy and Marilyn Manson did a version of Johnny B Good for the crowd. As I looked around the balcony, I saw the faces of a host of well-known stars staring back at me. Mick Jagger, The Corrs, The Edge, Alicia Silverstone and Sinead O'Connor all looked on and were, I'm sure, as shocked as I was to see the trio on the stage. Later, Bono hosted a massive party back in his Killiney home for the above-mentioned stars. Sadly, I wasn't invited.

Maybe coming to the end of a year makes people want to break up? Maybe it's to make a clean start for the New Year? Or maybe it's just that they don't want to buy their loved one a present for Christmas? Either way, coming to the end of 1999 everyone seemed to be breaking up. It seems they wanted to start the new millennium as single people and we were only too happy to record the facts for them. Jim Corr and the model Andrea Roche broke up. The Irish boxer Steve Collins and his wife Gemma split up. Miriam Ahern arrived at the Fianna Fáil Christmas dinner in the Burlington Hotel with both her daughters, while their father arrived with his girlfriend Celia. We knew it was going to be an interesting night. While everybody, including the guests, waited for a catfight, I caused terrible embarrassment to both Fianna Fáil and the Gardaí by breaking into the event without an invitation or a ticket.

The Taoiseach's VIP Christmas dinner is held for the great and the good of the party faithful, including all the Government ministers and their families plus a selection of stars for good measure. I had dressed in a tuxedo, and without receiving so much as a courtesy frisk, strolled passed the uniformed Gardaí at the door, passed the hotel's security guards, and into the ballroom passed Bertie's armed security. I stood beside him to say hello, much to his surprise. I then wrote about the whole incident in the paper and a lot of people were not happy bunnies. I even got a number of strange calls from those close to Bertie saying that they knew who I was and that's why I got so close to him. Now, if you believe that...

It wasn't all doom and gloom at the end of 1999. The former Riverdance star Jean Butler found love with the designer Cuan Hanley; Dunnes Stores heir Michael Heffernan married model Maureen Dolan; and I was trying to get together with the very sexy actress Angelica Huston, who was in town for the première of her new movie *Agnes Brown*. She prefers older, men it seems — men like her husband — so I took rejection well this time.

The year ended with us doing our first five months of the diary without even one lawsuit, something that Terry Keane's diary could not manage, judging by the amount of apologies each week in her column. The final diary of 1999 brought what some might call the story of the year from our esteemed editor Aengus Fanning. It was on how his friend and the papers' friend, former Miss Ireland, Olivia Tracey, had landed her first big acting role in the US after years of trying to make it as a blonde stunner in a city full of blonde stunners, most of whom were probably 20 years younger than she was — LA. Her big job was signed and sealed that week, as she announced via our column. She was to become the face for the advertising campaign to launch Viagra in America.

CHAPTER 8

A NEW MILLENNIUM —
PRIVATE JETS AND SUPERMODELS

(JANUARY–JUNE 2000)

With former Mrs Mick Jagger, model Jerry Hall

By the end of 1999 the world was getting ready to have the party of all parties. With the new millennium upon us, every type of bash was being organised by every type of person. With my newfound responsibility to the Sunday Indo, I volunteered to cover the new year celebrations on my own, as Gayle had gone away on holiday. It ended up being the most over-hyped night in history. We had been promised all types of great parties. Eddie Irvine flew in with a bunch of girls and a crate of champagne for a party in O'Reilly's bar under Tara Street station. The Taoiseach Bertie Ahern spent the day opening everything and anything to do with the new millennium, from the Millennium Lights under the bridges of the River Liffey to the Millennium Candle and, finally, the Millennium Concert, I attended them all and I'm sure Bertie thought I was stalking him, which, of course, I was.

The week after Christmas and just before New Year's Eve, I spent every waking moment running around Dublin to the opening of everything trying to get a story. I had to find out where everyone important was going to ring in the new year and the new millennium. Most of the interesting people were away so it was like trying to get blood out of a stone. I covered everything that week — big parties, small parties, outdoor marquee parties, country parties, parties abroad; everywhere was on my to-do list but the search was pretty much in vain.

On the night that was December 31, 1999 I set out to attend a private party thrown by former model Sonia Reynolds and her best friend and business partner Emma Kelly in their apartment. Then it was off to join Eddie Irvine and his crew in O'Reilly's before zipping down to meet my own friends in the VIP room of Annabel's nightclub in the Burlington Hotel, where the manager Joe Burns had given us our own area with as much champagne as the girls could drink. I, of course, got as much diet coke as I required. Not drinking alcohol was becoming a waste of a perfectly good perk of the job.

The new-year period was also the time when celebrity chef Conrad Gallagher started dating the one-time wife of Joe Elliot from Def Leppard, Karla. When a friend of Karla's told me she was going out with Conrad, it was such a perfect diary story that I actually could not believe it. The diary's two biggest stars hooking up was, to us, like getting six numbers and a bonus ball in the national lottery. Conrad now had big plans to open a new restaurant in Ballsbridge and was still running two other premises, including Lloyds Brassiere, just off Baggot Street. A while later, when his empire started to crumble, Conrad and all his staff were locked out of Lloyds when the landlord locked up the restaurant after rent payments were not made.

The following week, a story that was huge at the time just fell into my lap. At a gala dinner in Fitzpatrick's Hotel in Killiney, a man who had not been seen since the whole Terry Keane incident arrived out in public for the first time since Terry's famous 'Late Late Show' appearance. Former Taoiseach Charles J. Haughey had become a Howard Hughes type character in Ireland, disappearing from public view for most of the previous year ever since that fateful appearance by Terry. This event at the start of 2000 was one of the last times he would be seen socially before appearing at a string of tribunals of inquiry into various planning and financial irregularities, including his own financial affairs, and then putting his multimillion-pound home on the outskirts of Dublin up for sale. Haughey and his long-suffering wife Maureen were guests of the late, great hotelier Paddy Fitzpatrick. The Sunday Indo was over the moon that I got the story and photos of the couple out together, and celebrated with the headline "The return of the real first couple".

It also happened to be the same week I ran the story on Bertie's younger daughter, Cecelia, who had signed up to a new band who were trying to win a place representing Ireland in the Eurovision Song Contest. The band were called "Shimma" which is a tad like Shimmer, and I think that was the idea behind the name. The band had two guys, one blond girl and Cecilia. They didn't win and RTÉ came up with the great idea of the 'You're A Star' show, which now holds public auditions to find a suitable Eurovision entry for Ireland. For a country that has won the contest more than any other, ever since You're a Star started we have managed to do deplorably worse year after year.

Love was also in the air in January for Gavin Friday, famed more for being the best friend of Bono than for being the lead singer with the Seventies punk band The Virgin Prunes. In January, he hooked up with the British actress Anna Friel, star of TV soap 'Brookside' and a few films. They didn't last, especially after one of the tabloids rang the doorbell of Gavin's house and took Anna's photo when she opened the door in his dressing-gown, looking a tad the worse for wear.

Towards the end of January Bertie Ahern was in South Africa and so was Mary Harney (the Tánaiste). Thankfully, they were not there as a couple. Crona Byrne, Gay's daughter, started a short career with *Riverdance*. Def Leppard's Rick Savage (who had moved to Ireland to avail of tax breaks given on royalties to songwriters) and his girlfriend announced they were having a baby and getting married. The Cork actor and star of the movie *Michael Collins*, Jonathan Rhys-Myers, broke up with his girlfriend, actress Toni Colette, star of *Muriel's Wedding*. So it was just another humdrum week in the world of gossip.

The current Miss Ireland, Emir Holohan Doyle, hooked up very briefly with the comedian Daire O'Briain. Then only a week after breaking up with Toni Colette, Jonathan Rhys-Myers hooked up with the Dublin model Cha Cha Seigne (yes, that is a real name). Actor John Hurt held the first decent bash of 2000 with all the Irish stars that were at the opening of his latest play in London, Samuel Beckett's *Krapp's Last Tape*. Later, he would move the play to Dublin, where Michael Colgan put it in the Gate Theatre for a sell-out run. At the London première of the play guests included Eddie Jordan (during a time when he still owned a racing team), Chris de Burgh (at a time before his daughter was Miss World), and comedian Dave Allen (at the time when he was still alive).

Bono was getting ready for a massive house party full of supermodels in his Killiney pad, and all with his wife's permission. His wife, Ali Hewson, was running the Supermodels Fashion Show in The Point theatre the following month, and a host of stars, such as Christy Turlington, Kate Moss, Naomi Campbell, the Rolling Stone Ron Wood, Yasmin Le Bon, Eva Herzegovina and Jerry Hall, were all expected to make an appearance.

February started with Michael Flatley in the White House supporting Hillary Clinton's campaign to get elected to the Senate. Conrad Gallagher was telling anyone who would listen that he was about to move his new girlfriend Karla Elliot into his new million-pound house in Killiney once it was finished. It never did get finished, and was, in fact, repossessed. He was also about to launch his new restaurant, Ocean, down by the docks. Well, he was running the kitchen side of things down there, but the relationship between Conrad and the owners soured very quickly.

I cheered myself up by bringing Emir Holohan Doyle, the current

Miss Ireland, to the première of the new Neil Jordan movie *The End of the Affair*. She looked stunning, and the star of the première, Ralph Fiennes, spent the night chatting to her on my behalf, or so he told me. Shortly afterwards, I got to spend the night in the Merrion Hotel with my very own Spice Girl. Okay, so it was only Sporty Spice, the lesbian icon, but it was a fun interview. We spent an hour in her suite talking about her career after The Spice Girls split.

With Sport Spice, Melanie C in her hotel room of the Merrion hotel. Pic.: David Conachy

A week later, it was time for the big fashion show and there were supermodels everywhere. I watched Bono and Mick Jagger watching Mick's ex-wife Jerry Hall on the catwalk at The Point theatre. Shortly before that night, Mick had been forced to pay Jerry $10 million in their divorce settlement. I'm sure that was the subject of their conversation. The only thing on people's minds that week was the fashion show, as Ireland isn't used to seeing supermodels all over its streets. It was really the only party in town, and it was paradise for every gossip columnist.

Eddie Jordan, Ron Wood, actors Patrick Bergin and Jason Priestly, singer Natalie Imbruglia, U2, John Rocha, Patrick Kielty, Amanda Byram, Simply Red's Mick Hucknall, Simon Le Bon, boxer Chris Eubank, the former Formula One driver Damon Hill, The Corrs and Chris Evans were all there, and that was just the front row. It was the first big party of the year and after the show VIP parties were everywhere. Well, mostly everywhere I couldn't get into.

U2's hotel, The Clarence, was where the main party was on. Within that party were sub-parties, depending on how famous you were. The VVVIPs were in Bono's private bash in the penthouse suite of the hotel, and the plain old VVIPs were in another private bash in the hotel's restaurant.

The last week of February saw the première of the hit play *The Beauty Queen of Leenane* in the Gaiety theatre. It was one of the few premières that I actually enjoyed. It was jammed with stars, including the new hot couple around town, singer Sinead O'Connor and the former gossip columnist Dermott Hayes.

Bono's wife Ali Hewson was attending the play with Bono's friend Gavin Friday, while nearby later that night Bono was out on the town with Andrea Corr and Mick Jagger.

Bono chatting during one of our good days. Pic.: John Dardis

U2 were still the biggest story in town and number one on my list for good showbiz stories. I got a pass to attend a show they were doing in the Astoria in London for 2,000 lucky fans and I was planning to attend their world tour in Miami later in the year. Suddenly, my ticket was taken away from me by U2's publicity company. I never knew why, but I must have done something very wrong? After I kicked up stink, my editor got a call from Paul McGuiness, the band's manager about me. So, I decided to move on and leave them alone for the moment.

It was also the same week that the former Miss Ireland, Amanda Brunker started a fling with the Simply Red singer Mick Hucknall. Amanda, who was later exposed for having an affair with the married actor James Nesbitt, star of the TV show 'Cold Feet', flew to Paris for a weekend with Hucknall. The relationship didn't last. Amanda has since become a journalist and television starlet. Furthermore, she has always been fun to be around and never takes herself too seriously. She even takes her mother Betty to all the posh parties and has great fun with everyone. I just wish more people in the media were like her.

My final scoop of February was finally to interview Celia Larkin. I tried to get an interview with the woman who was sharing a bed with the leader of Ireland but had failed time after time. So one day I just called her on her house phone and by luck she picked it up herself. I wanted to ask her about her new career as a beauty consultant. She seemed to know more about me than I knew about her. She asked me all about stories she had read in the column. She asked about my website, which I was planning to launch, and by the end of the phone call she had actually interviewed me before I got the chance to get any gossip from her. Then, she hung up and I had just been conned by the first girlfriend.

Only weeks later I went to a party with Cecelia Ahern. It was the week that a row erupted in the press claiming that both daughters of our esteemed leader refused to walk out with Celia and Bertie during his party's annual conference. Cecelia rubbished the reports and also admitted to me that she was giving up her career as a wannabe pop star and going back to college to study journalism. Years later, she would graduate and become a famed novelist.

I could see why Cecelia didn't want to spend her life running around town chasing celebrities, like I did on a daily basis. Being a novelist is a much better way to earn a living then hanging around nightclubs waiting for some star to get to drunk and do something stupid. However, in my defence, it was a life that seemed to change on a day-to-day basis and that was the way I liked it. One day, it was covering U2 getting the freedom of the city, the next it was Michael Flatley announcing a wedding date with his girlfriend. Then it was finding out who Chris Evans would be having as a guest on his TFI television show, which he was bringing to Dublin for St Patrick's Day.

During St Patrick's week, Puff Daddy, the rap mogul, was back in town again. The star was without his then girlfriend Jennifer Lopez and with an entourage who drank nearly £10,000 worth of champagne during a wild party in Lillies. After his concert in The Point theatre, they headed to the club and from there back to the Merrion Hotel with a fleet of cars filled with girls for a party that went on until 7am. Without going to bed, Puffy then left the party to fly to Frankfurt. Now, that's rock and roll.

By the end of March, I was still trying to get Celia back for tricking me on the phone. So while she was with Bertie in Australia, I bought the name www.CeliaLarkin.com on the internet for £20. Now she could not open a website under her own name. It was childish but funny, and to top it off we announced in the paper that Celia could buy the name back from me if she wanted, but she didn't. I was also still trying to get back into Bono's good graces. In early April I thought that doing a story that had been kept secret might get me back on Bono's good side: it was a story on how U2 had been up for the freedom of the city 10 years before they got it. In 1990, Fianna Fáil councillors had rejected a vote to give U2 the freedom of the city because of Bono's political views. Bono and U2 didn't seem to care.

From the first week in April I was a pretty busy boy with the influx of stars, all of whom I was trying to get some good showbiz stories on. The week started with a lunch with the singer Bryan Ferry, an after-show party with Macy Gray (who I think was in for the Heineken Green Energy festival) and a date with some model whose name I don't even remember. That's happens a lot with me and models, who are mostly dull and boring and always bad in bed.

The Celia Larkin website thing had grown and grown. Although she didn't want to buy her website name back from me, she was far from happy when she heard that someone else had bought www.bertieahern.com and directed it to a pornographic website.

Bertie's ex-wife Miriam, who had become a close friend of mine, was selling the Ahern family home in Malahide for a new place in Swords and a country home in Wexford. The same week, a movie about the life of James Joyce, *Nora*, premièred in Dublin, with stars such as Kate Moss and Sadie Frost arriving in for the party. Sadie was then married to an unknown young actor called Jude Law. I always wonder what happened to him...

Our old enemy John Ryan hadn't gone away either. He was back, and this time in partnership with the first girlfriend Celia Larkin on his new magazine called *TV Now*. She was going to be a columnist in the new magazine, and so the war between John Ryan and myself ignited yet again. It was John and Celia in one corner and myself and Miriam in the other. At the launch of *VIP* magazine he had actually squared up to me in the lift of the Fitzwilliam Hotel. Nothing happened, but it was very funny, as I was shorter and much bigger than John, while he was skinny and much taller than me. We looked like Little and Large standing toe to toe, staring into each other's eyes. Well, I was staring into his chest and he was staring at the top of my head.

That was also the same week that the Oscar-winning actress Gwyneth Paltrow arrived in Ireland. She was visiting the tiny village of Adare in County Limerick, where her best friend was getting married. The Oscar-winner then flew to Dublin for a night in U2's Clarence Hotel, before flying back to LA. The manager of the Dunraven Arms Hotel in Adare, where Gwyneth was staying, had a good idea. He got a photo of himself with her while she was at the hotel and sent me the photo. Now, unlike these silly hoteliers who say, "I'm not asking my guest for a photo", it was a very smart move. It was a photo that would be seen by over a million people in the Sunday Indo. It cost nothing and got lots of publicity. The star didn't mind, and remember, there is no such thing as bad publicity.

At the end of April I broke the story that Pierce Brosnan was getting married on May 20 in Ashford Castle. Brosnan's publicist in LA was still keeping me abreast of things and everything was ready to go. The actor was already in Ireland filming the indoor scenes for his new movie *The Tailor of Panama* with the Ireland-based director John Boorman.

Boorman's house guest was the actress Jamie Lee Curtis, who was also Brosnan's co-star in the movie. It was coming up to Brosnan's birthday, so I dropped him in a case of champagne, which my friend Tara O'Connor, who worked in PR for the champagne brand, got him as a gift from the company. It had a card wishing him happy birthday from them and requesting an interview from me. Sadly, he never got it. The very night I dropped it off, Brosnan flew out to LA where his son had been involved in a car accident. Thankfully, his son was fine, but the wedding had to be moved to later that year.

It was also time for the Punchestown races. I got stories and interviewed anyone who was in attendance, from supermodel Jasmine Guinness to the former Taoiseach Albert Reynolds. A week later, Bono turned 40, and Andrea Corr wasn't talking to me, claiming that I knew too much about her and nothing to do with the fact she turned me down for a coffee only a year before, when I had cheekily asked her out on a date. Bono celebrated his fortieth with his close friends on a whirlwind around-the-world party which, of course, ended up in Dublin's Renards nightclub at 4am.

One Saturday night in mid-May I got a call from my editor, Anne

Harris. She said that the Minister for Sport, Jim McDaid, had been spotted with a blonde in a bar in Monkstown and would I go out to have a look. It was 9pm on a Saturday night, and I got in my car and was at the bar within 20 minutes. McDaid was separated and a bit of a playboy around town. When I arrived in the bar, the Minister turned and saw me. His only words were "Oh shit", as the blonde said to him "Of all the people". Then, to my amazement, Jim grabbed the blonde, finished his drink and ran out the door and down the road. As I walked out the door of the bar, I watched as the Minister skipped down the road with this lady friend in order to get away from me. It had to be one of the funniest things I had ever witnessed.

This was also the month when everyone seemed to be either making up or breaking up, and, as usual, I documented every detail in the Sunday Indo. The actress Victoria Smurfit got married; the former Miss Ireland, Amanda Brunker broke up with yet another semi-famous boyfriend; and Eddie Irvine broke up with his girlfriend Anouk, whom he had dated for a whole year.

Rumours were also circulating that the story of an Irish Notting Hill-type movie was in the works. The story was based on the friendship between the Oscar-winning actress Julia Roberts and the Irish chauffeur Mick Devine. I have rarely written about Mick because he hates it passionately, so I will only write what is known within the media of their friendship.

Years ago, when Julia was just starting out and was dating Kiefer Sutherland, they came to Dublin and stayed in the Shelbourne Hotel. They had a fight and Julia left the hotel. Not knowing anyone in Dublin she rang her driver, Mick Devine. It was early in the morning and Julia was upset, so Mick took her to his house — a three-bed semi in the Dublin suburb of Palmerstown. Well, where else could have taken her?

Julia then spent two weeks with Mick's family, and months later she brought the driver and his family to LA to stay in her house.

In 2003, when Julia met her husband-to-be Danny Moder, she brought him to Ireland to meet Mick and his family. With Julia's father having passed away, Mick was asked by the star to give her away when she finally married Danny in LA. While it all ended up happily ever after for them, the film never got made so we never got a story.

Things were also not going well for our old friend Conrad Gallagher. He had pulled out of his latest venture, a restaurant called Mango Toast in the Fitzwilliam Hotel. He also finished his partnership with the new Ocean bar and restaurant. Then, in a blaze of publicity, his Lloyds restaurant was closed down. Conrad, however, was still talking to the press with his then girlfriend Karla, both claiming they had got engaged.

At the start of June, Conrad was getting very diva-like. He told one photographer who wanted to take his photo that he only had 10 seconds in which to take it. To which the snapper replied, "Well, I only have five, so get on with it". The big fall for Conrad was on its way and we were only too happy to see it coming. His behaviour had gone beyond funny and he was starting to become very rude and ignorant. The press were getting bored with him, and when you are up as high as Conrad was and start pissing people off, there is only one way you can go and that's down.

I was on RTÉ television at the end of June, as the legendary 2FM DJ Dave Fanning went on holidays from his Sunday morning show that was broadcast simultaneously on TV and radio. For the two weeks Dave was away his showbiz presenter Bianca Luykx took over Dave's position as the presenter while I took over her position as the showbiz presenter. I was getting more and more TV jobs and at that stage had done 'Open House', 'Fish' (a kid's music and pop show) and even a few showbiz slots on TV3's early-morning breakfast show. But the 6am starts killed me.

CHAPTER 9

WOULD YOU LIKE TO DANCE, MR FLATLEY?

(JULY–DECEMBER 2000)

Michael Flatley shows me the best way to pose on the sun bed. Pic.: Brian McAvoy

The last six months of 2000 were, unfortunately, far from exciting in the world of gossip in Ireland but we soldiered on despite this minor issue. Michael Flatley was on and off again with the Tallaght Temptress. He invited me to Budapest in Hungary to see the opening night of his new show, and then failed to turn up to the party after. We did, however, dance in the green room backstage. Then, when his PA came in and announced that the Prime Minister of Hungary was waiting outside to meet him, Flatley said, "Let him wait. Jason has come all the way from Ireland." You have to love him.

Due to time-restrictions, and being unable to leave the paper mid-week as we were in the middle of doing the diary, I had to fly into Hungary one morning and fly out the following evening. During my one day in the country, I got to spend the day in the Turkish Baths in Budapest, and soon realised that I had a big gay following. But that is a story for another day.

Flatley gets shown how we waltz in downtown Dublin. Pic.: Brian McAvoy

Back in Ireland, I chased day-to-day stories on the diary. The Irish television star Twink started and ended a new dating show on TV3 called 'Perfect Match'. It wasn't actually a perfect match at all and was cancelled. Bertie's daughter Cecelia was playing tennis at a charity event with stars such as Ilie Nastase. Thankfully, to break the boredom, Gayle got the story that Shane Filan from Westlife was secretly dating a girl called Gillian, who was the cousin of Kian from the band. Shane denied it, the record company denied it and Louis Walsh denied it. Today, they are married. Chris Evans was back in town for a game of golf and donated $50,000 to Ronan Keating's cancer charity. He also tried to buy U2's hotel, but Bono said no.

During the Witness music festival I got a chance to interview Nicole Appleton from the band All Saints. The only way I got the interview was by hanging around the toilets outside her dressing-room. She refused to talk about her new boyfriend, Liam Gallagher from Oasis but I had already met him once. It was in the toilets of a Dublin hotel. I was washing my hands and as I turned around, he was coming out of the cubicle behind me still wearing his sunglasses. When he went back to the bar, a number of journalists and myself waited near him but every one of us refused to approach him for fear of getting the shit kicked out of us. This was something Liam liked to do to members of the press from time to time.

With Nicole Appleton backstage and away from Liam Gallagher

Soon after that Eddie Irvine was back in Dublin with his new-look bleached hair. Gabriel Byrne moved back to Ireland to enjoy his new house on Baggot Street. He told friends he was thinking of giving up acting; thankfully, he didn't.

In September Bono was back on the streets and secretly walking around Dublin filming a short movie called Sightings of Bono. The movie didn't win any Academy Awards. Bono then hosted a party for the band REM in Conrad Gallagher's Peacock Alley restaurant, and even paid the $6,000 bill for guests, which included the supermodel Helena Christensen.

Emma Buckley replaced Amanda Byram on TV3, and Dermot Desmond, the businessman who owns most of Glasgow Celtic Football Club, bought fashion designer Sybil Connolly's old house on Merrion Square for £6 million. Don Baker, the musician, split up with his wife, the actress Lorraine Pilkington got engaged, and Ted Kennedy, JFK's brother, hosted a dinner in the City West Hotel.

Then came news we were all waiting for — Karla Elliott broke up with Conrad Gallagher and then started dating the 70-year-old beef baron David Doane. Jean Butler, the former *Riverdance* star, lost close to £3 million on her own version of *Riverdance* called *Dancing on Dangerous Ground*. It had obviously been very dangerous for her. I flew to London for the opening night, and could see why it didn't last. It didn't have the pulling power Riverdance had and was missing the likes of Flatley to wow the crowd.

Miriam Ahern started to come out more and more in public, and even danced the night away in the Morrison Hotel with Mr Ireland, Padraig Hearn, at the Westlife album launch. Every nugget of gossip coming my way went into a variety of publications. First was the Sunday Indo column, which got every exclusive story — always. Next was ShowbizIreland.com, my website, which needed to be updated five days a week. Then there were the weekly radio slots. Finally, there were the monthly magazine columns I did: one in the women's magazine *U*; the other in the cultural magazine *Food & Wine*.

For some reason I become the face of the Nizoral anti-dandruff shampoo

About this time I was approached by a company representing the shampoo Nizoral. It was an anti-dandruff product that was aimed at the young and hip market with an advertising campaign about hitting the social scene. They asked me if I would put my name to the product if they ran a caption saying, "Ireland's biggest gossip columnist and showbiz reporter knows that first impressions are important. Appearance is everything if you want to be a mover and shaker in Dublin's fair city." I asked did I have to do anything and they said not really, just get them a photo and agree the fee. Without a doubt, it was the easiest money I've ever made.

Bono held a party in November for his father's birthday, and kicked if off with a karaoke session in The Clarence Hotel. His father didn't want Bono to sing, as the rock star admitted: "He always thought I was a bit of a show-off".

By mid-November I was in Sweden at the MTV awards. I was lucky enough to sit next to Louis Walsh on the plane going over. He invited me to ride with him to the awards in his limo. When we arrived at the stadium where the awards were on, I stayed with Louis and went backstage, where he got me an access-all-areas pass for the night.

I then went into the press room to rub Paul Martin's face in it with my pass, and spent the night live on radio in Dublin via my mobile phone talking to all the stars backstage. Ronan Keating, The Edge from U2, Moloko and the Backstreet Boys were all interviewed over my phone. It was amazing. I was even backstage beside Kylie Minogue when Madonna turned up on stage with a T-shirt that had Kylie's name on it. Kylie started hugging everyone. Well, everyone except me.

Ricky Martin walked past me and I remember thinking: "very bad skin". Robbie Williams had his dressing-room door open and was getting his hair sprayed to within an inch of its life. Jennifer Lopez was wandering around with her entourage of dancers. Kelis walked into me and apologised, she was barely known in the music scene at that stage; I commented on how great she looked and she politely said "thank you" and moved on. Anastasia drank a bottle of coke surrounded by two huge black guys. Could be dancers, could be bodyguards or one could even be her boyfriend. I didn't stop to ask. When I got home, I wrote a great four-page spread for *U* magazine. Definitely one of my best. After the awards, I lost Louis and Ronan, whose dressing-room I had been hanging out in. I went to a few parties, but they were all crap, so I rang Paul Martin and crashed on his hotel-room floor. A perfect example of how you can go from being a king to a pauper in a matter of minutes in the world of show business.

At the end of November, Miriam Ahern and Celia Larkin came face to face for the first time when someone invited Miriam as their guest to the Jen Kelly fashion show. Nobody at the event knew Miriam was going, and Celia (a friend of Jen's) was there to do something for RTÉ. They were kept on different floors, and the only man going between them was the Deputy Lord Mayor of Dublin, Royston Brady, who was friends with both ladies and was left trying to keep the peace. You could cut the tension with a knife but we got a great story when we spotted Celia using a Government car for her work with RTÉ. A week later Miriam was my guest at the Sinatra ball and she was a delight to have for the night. All my mates thought she was a lovely lady.

At the beginning of December I was asked to do another monthly magazine column for a lady who was paying good money but whose idea was a tad odd. She wanted to launch a magazine based on the *Hello!/OK!* style, not just about stars and their homes, but about stars in their homes with their pets. The magazine was called TLC (tender loving care.) It didn't last long. I always wondered why...

The actor Mickey Rourke was buying a home in Ireland and Ronan Keating and his wife were announcing via our column that they were having a second baby. Model Jemma Kidd was hanging out with Eddie Irvine and for the first time in the paper's history, we were in colour.

Celia and Miriam both came out fighting and both made careers for themselves in the battle for Bertie Ahern. Planet Hollywood was closed and sold off to a bar chain. The couple who had spent £7 million on Ireland's most expensive house in Killiney had still not moved in three years later due to planning issues.

Who was to know that our last column of 2000 would have a story about Jim Corr and Andrea Roche, the former Miss Ireland, which would land the Gardaí at her door and nearly land me in hospital?

CHAPTER 10

THE INCIDENT OF THE GLASS AND THE MODEL
(JANUARY–JUNE 2001)

A photo taken of my head after being hit by a glass by the former Miss Ireland Andrea Roche

It was an average night in Lillies when the incident involving Andrea Roche and myself occurred. By the end of the week, it would end up on the front pages of the tabloids and all over the radio.

It all started in one of my final columns of 2000 when I wrote about the romance between Andrea Roche and Jim Corr. It was edited as usual by the diary team, who regularly changed my prose to make it more diary-like. In my opening line about Andrea and Jim, I said something about Andrea Roche having gone one step closer in her desire to become Andrea Corr. It then said, in brackets, "no, she hasn't lost two stone and learned to sing". I didn't notice the additional line when I proofread it; then again, I am a man who would pay no attention to details like that about a woman's weight. I thought Andrea Roche had a great figure, and the comment was more directed at Andrea Corr being too skinny. Ms Roche, however, took the comment to heart, so much so that a short while later in Lillies she approached me, very upset about the comments I had written. She threw a drink over me, then another, and then she grabbed a third glass to throw its contents over me too. The glass slipped out of her hand, probably due to her hands being wet from the first two thrown drinks. The glass smashed into my forehead — however, with the size of my forehead, it's pretty hard to miss. I was in shock and my head was starting to bleed. The fun had gone out of the joke and I immediately got the management who took Ms Roche aside and took me downstairs to get my cut seen to.

As I had my eyes closed and was getting a paper stitch put on, Roche came down the stairs and slapped me in the face. Well, that was it. She was asked to leave the club and soon afterwards I got in my car and drove up to Harcourt Terrace Garda Station, where I reported the assault and gave them Roche's mobile number.

The following morning a friend of mine, Ken Murray, who worked for the radio news agency INN, rang me and asked me about a rumour he had heard about the incident. I said, "Ken, I really can't comment about Andrea Roche hitting me in the head with a glass last night in Lillies as the matter is with the police in Harcourt Terrace, where it was reported last night. OK?" He got the message. On the lunchtime news, a report came out on the radio that a journalist had been assaulted by a model in a Dublin nightclub the night before. An hour later, the next report said it was the former Miss Ireland, Andrea Roche who had assaulted the journalist in Lillies. The next hour they had my name, and the story in full was out. Both *The Mirror* and *The Star* ran the story the following day and my phone was ringing so much that my battery died within two hours. In the end, I didn't follow the up case as I thought Andrea had been embarrassed enough by the incident. Today, we get on fine, but back then I think it was a wake-up call for her to stop partying so much.

The new year was off to a flying start and the Celtic Tiger was in full swing. Everybody had money and wanted everybody else to know it. Unknown to me, Gayle was planning on make the move to *Ireland on Sunday* for a big pile of cash, rumoured to be double what the Sunday Indo was paying her. I had turned down a few offers from the paper. I just thought that in time the Sindo would give me the column on my own. Like most years the stars all rang in the new year in far-flung places. Bertie Ahern was in Spain on holiday, Eddie Irvine was in Bali, Michael Flatley was in Vienna, and just about everyone else in Lillies or Renards.

Miriam Ahern was enjoying her new-found celebrity on a skiing trip to Switzerland; model Alison Canavan had split with the Dunnes Stores heir Andrew Heffernan; supermodel Jasmine Guinness was pregnant; and Louis Walsh was spinning yarns again about Samantha Mumba going for dinner in London with Eminem — again we wrote about it and again we were stitched up. Supermodel Sophie Dahl, the new face of just about everything and one of the world's best-known models, was in Dublin to launch a new magazine called *The Dubliner*. She told me an interesting story about a thing called "'a spinner". Baffled, I asked her what it was. She said it was a girl who was so small that she could sit on top of a man during sex and do a 360-degree turn. I was impressed.

Down in the Morrison Hotel, the actor, Matthew McConaughey was in residence during the filming of possibly the worst film ever made in Ireland. It was being filmed down in Ardmore studios and was called *Reign of Fire*. Matt was in Dublin for months during filming and struck up a good friendship with the Irish boxer Jim Rock, who helped train him for the movie. Matt was so taken with the boxer that he actually attended Jim's wedding. The film's other main star was Christian Bale, who is the lead in the new Batman movie. The two of them spent ages in Dublin, but the end result was the biggest turkey of the year and was so bad that when I went to the première I actually walked out.

McConaughey, who was once interviewed by the police for playing the drums naked in his home and causing the neighbours to complain about the noise, spent most of his time in Ireland training with Rock. Bale took a house with his wife for the duration of film but rarely made public appearances. I met him at the première but he is extremely quiet and hates the press. McConaughey hates the media too, and never hit any of Dublin's trendy clubs during filming. He just worked, trained and enjoyed the company of boxers.

The Holywood actor Matthew McCounaghey at the National Boxing stadium with Jim Rock. Pic.: Gerry McDonald

By the start of February 2001, I was getting ready to celebrate my twenty-eighth birthday. However, I wasn't going to be celebrating it in the new salon of Dylan Bradshaw, stylist to The Corrs, who was having a party with a host of VIPs. Dylan had the great idea of "not" inviting our diary team to the opening of the salon. Instead, he got his PR person to tell us we were barred, as Dylan thought his clients would feel uncomfortable in our presence. I was so pissed off at the time, but now, years later and looking back, I guess it was a smart move. Why invite journalists who would take the piss and drink your free champagne? In the process, you would only annoy stars such as The Corrs who pay you silly amounts of money to be their stylist.

2001 was also the year I went to my first and only Brit Awards in London. What a waste of space! Being in the Irish press, as I have so often ranted, gives you fuck-all access in the UK. They treat you like shite. I covered the *Lord of the Rings* première in the UK and was treated like an alien by the London PR company running the event. I only got into that movie because a friend of mine from *The Sunday People* didn't bother going and gave me his passes. If it was not for him, I would have been left out in the cold, freezing my ass off because I worked for an Irish newspaper.

With Samanta Mumba trying my Tarzan pulling technique. Pic.: John Dardis

Anyway, back at the Brit awards in Earls Court in London, I eventually got my accreditation. It would have been easier to have a chart-topping album and get in as a star guest than it was to go as a journalist from Ireland. When I did get inside the theatre I took it that it would be like all the MTV awards I had attended. Stars would get their awards then pop into the press room to do some questions.

U2 were topping the bill, and guests also included Westlife. When I arrived I was sent backstage. I thought this would be great fun until I realised that backstage was literally backstage. It was a small office with a TV, where we were expected to stay for the entire night and watch the awards on a screen. No access to the stars, no interviews, no nothing.

I was furious and ready to hit someone. I walked out after 20 minutes and told the monkey of a security guard that I was going to the toilet. I walked right to the front of the stage and watched the show. Once it was over, I found Westlife manager Louis Walsh and the boss of Universal Records in Ireland, Dave Pennyfeather. They got me into the Universal party, where Louis met up with the singer Samantha Mumba, whom I barely knew at that stage. She was wearing this slip of a black dress that got her on the cover of every paper the next day.

Louis was entertaining and networking the room, and he asked me to take care of Samantha for him. I was only overjoyed to do it. The Irish comedian Graham Norton walked by us and I told him everybody said I looked like a butch version of him. He responded with "Darling, imagine how I feel", and walked away. When Louis returned he walked Samantha and myself over to a private room where U2 were having a party and I walked in hand in hand with Samantha. The was more to do with the fact that she couldn't walk in her heels than anything romantic.

Bono at the Brits awards on stage only a short while before he had me thrown out of the after-party

As soon as Bono saw me he grabbed Louis and told him to get me out. I knew there was no point in fighting with the biggest rock star in the world at a party which was organised by his record company, so I left. After all, it was a party I was not supposed to be attending in the first place. I waited outside until Louis emerged and he let me join him and Westlife at another party in Home House, where one of the coolest Brit Awards parties was going on.
I got out of the taxi and watched while the boys got bombarded with flashes from hundreds of paparazzi cameras. It was a surreal experience as Westlife's bodyguard Paul Higgins came down to the door to let me in. Once inside, everywhere you looked you saw famous faces. It was dark and jungle-style dance music was playing. Dancers and stylists were thrown among the hoards of stars, A-listers, B-listers and even a few C-listers. I sat and chatted to Shane and Nicky from Westlife and then I was lucky enough to introduce them to Mark Owen who used to be in the band, Take That. I had met Mark at the Witness festival in Punchestown a few months before. Mark had been wandering around on his own at this rock festival and nobody had even noticed him. We had shared a drink and a chat before, so when I got to the party with Westlife he approached me to say hello and the boys were over the moon.

They told Mark how the members of Take That had been their heroes when they were growing up in Sligo. Mark told them that Westlife were the band of the moment and they should enjoy it. It was very humbling to be sitting with two of the biggest boy bands from the past 20 years and chatting about how they both admired each other. Then it all come to a head briefly as Paul McGuinness, U2's manager, saw me and went mad. Louis calmed him down, as Paul was clearly not happy to see me at the party.

At around 4am Westlife got ready to leave and dropped me off at my hotel on the way. It was a tad weird as I listened to Paul Higgins ring their hotel and get the back door opened using passwords like "Mr Smith and Goldilocks are on the way. Can you open the back entrance?"

Back in Dublin it was time for the press photographer's awards which were being held in UCD. It was always a night I enjoyed as, for some reason, I always got on better with photographers than journalists. I felt they (like me) were out on the street working and not tied to a desk drinking lattes, like most people who did my job.

Actor Gabriel Byrne shows his enthusiasm at the prospect of being interviewed by me. Pic.: John Dardis

Guests on the night included the actor Gabriel Byrne and Sir Bob Geldof, both of whom I admired hugely, and both of whom have always been totally professional with me. Geldof once gave me advice on how to make money from my website by telling me always to listen to the marketing people. Sadly, I didn't have any, so that idea was out the window. Byrne always held a special place in my heart, as he was the most famous person ever to come from Walkinstown in Dublin, where I grew up.

I knew at this stage that my Bono issues had to be addressed. After he had had me thrown out of party at the Brit Awards in London, I knew things were going to get worse for our relationship before they got better. And boy was I right.

CHAPTER 11

BREAKING INTO THE BOND WEDDING

(JULY–DECEMBER 2001)

During one of our many interviews. Pierce Brosnan never forgets the Irish press. Pic.: Mark Doyle

The summer of 2001 was the one that got everybody talking. For me, it started with a trip to New York, where I was subjected to another night on the town with Michael Flatley. He was opening his show in Madison Square Gardens, and yet again he flew a few lucky journalists over for the trip. The trip was marred by rumours that Flatley was being stalked and that the FBI had been called. Nobody would comment officially on it, but to this day I feel it might have been a publicity thing. There was no way to prove it was, though, and his show was amazing. Afterwards Flatley held a party with all the show's dancers plus a lot of his family, who had flown in from Chicago.

Michael is very proud of his Irish roots. Although he was born in America, both his parents are Irish and one gets the feeling from Flatley that he wishes he was Irish too. So, with no proof of his stalker, we settled for one hell of a party with his parents after the show. He was single again and flirting with every dancer on the show. His reputation for being a ladies' man is one that (in my view) is far from being just a rumour. Some see Michael as sleazy.

He is, just a little, but in the nicest possible way.

Once I got back to Dublin, it was business as usual. Ciara Ferguson had started to work on the diary and was getting stuck in after Gayle had left. I was now also working on *WHO* magazine and things were going well. The magazine had started in April when I got a phone call from the publisher Mike Hogan. Never one to mince his words or hang around, Mike told me he was starting an Irish showbiz magazine and wanted me as the showbiz editor.

In March 2000, I had started ShowbizIreland.com with my friend Ray Senior. I had originally wanted to do Irish showbiz stories and sell them around the world. Ray, who was a website designer, talked me into doing it on the web, and the site was born. Over the next few years, it would just keep getting bigger and bigger. Today Ray runs VipIreland.com, Ireland's biggest paparazzi website and makes a fortune selling shots to most of the magazines around the world.

Our fake press cards for ShowBizIreland.com so we could get into parties and concerts for free

For me, I couldn't have been busier. On top of the Sunday Indo, *WHO* and the website, the BBC had asked me about doing a show called 'Fish out of Water'. It had been commissioned by the channel and was going to be filmed in September. The show's angle was that I would take over the role of a reporter for the *Portadown Times* and spend a week covering local news in Northern Ireland, while their reporter would come down to *WHO* magazine and cover my job for a week, interviewing celebrities and going to A-list parties.

On July 7 I was on the road again and driving down to the tiny village of Cratloe in County Limerick. The reason for my trip was the wedding of the fiddle player from The Corrs, Sharon, to the barrister Gavin Bonner. The couple had always been charming to deal with and their wedding showed other stars how to have a celebrity wedding without any bad press. There were no *Hello!* magazine photographers, no burly bodyguards and no mass hysteria. They arrived with their family. The only stars at the wedding were Patrick Kielty and Amanda Byram. The party afterwards was in Dromoland Castle. As the couple posed for the press outside the church, none of us had any need to try and break in. The whole event was media-free, except for a few photographers. I guess that's the way most people want the most important day of their life to be. The day was about them and not about the media, and I applaud them for that.

Mid-July was a busy time for me, as we did more stories on how the son of the Irish golfer Peter Townsend had started to date a little-known actress called Charlize Theron. As I mentioned earlier, the young actor's name was Stuart Townsend and the couple had met on a low-budget movie called *24 Hours* and have been madly in love ever since. A year or two later I tried to get a scoop about his brother Dylan Townsend trying to break into the world of modelling. It would have made a good story, but Dylan wasn't very media-savvy and missed the opportunity. So the story died.

Bertie Ahern's younger daughter had also found love with a young athlete called David Keoghan. Cecelia was very publicity-shy, as was David, but they posed for photos at one of the premières for the new *Star Wars* movie, and that's really all you can ask of a young couple who want to stay out of the public eye.

John Ryan was back on my radar at the end of July, as I heard that he was going to sell up his shares in *VIP* magazine and go out on his own as a publisher. He wanted to start a gay magazine called *GI*, which he did and which lasted a few months. Then he went on to start a terrible Sunday paper called *Stars on Sunday*.

Stars on Sunday actually lasted for only six weeks. It was just a collection of photos taken from all the week's events, stuck together in a cheap free-sheet-style paper which John had the cheek to sell for €1. The events covered in the paper were trendy fashion shows. The companies that would normally advertise in publications that covered these types of events tended to be highbrow brands like Louis Vuitton and Gucci. The problem for John was that as the paper looked cheap, no highbrow brands would advertise in it. Within weeks it folded. Some years later John would try his hand again at magazines when he moved to New York. He started *The New York Dog*, a magazine for New York's dog-lovers. Apparently, sales are getting better, year by year.

With Sharon Corr's wedding out of the way, I was looking forward to Pierce Brosnan's big day, which was set to go ahead on August 4. He had sold the rights of the wedding to *Hello!* magazine and just breaking the story that the wedding was going ahead was not enough for me. I would have to get in and I had just two weeks to plan it.

By July 22, I was chasing the actress Drew Barrymore around Dublin. She had got married to the American comedian Tom Green, and the couple had come to Ireland on their honeymoon — God knows why. They were spotted in Saint Stephen's Green and then went on to enjoy lunch in a tiny café on Merrion Row which was then known as Kitty's Kaboodle. The name came from the World War I saying to have your "kit and kaboodle", also known as your army kit. Kitty's was a restaurant I helped open with the owner Sil Costello a year or two before I went to study journalism. He had plagued me for years to write about the restaurant, and the one day that a Hollywood star goes into it I read about it afterwards in *The Sun*. Drew and Tom's marriage lasted only a little longer than their honeymoon: the couple split soon after they returned from Ireland to LA.

A few days later it was time to head to Galway for Brosnan's wedding. I put my plan into action: on the day before the wedding,

I got two friends to come with me down to Ashford Castle where the wedding was taking place. Derek Daly, a friend from Killarney, had a convertible BMW and he drove both myself and my other friend Padraig Hearns down to the castle, with me sitting in the back seat. As we got closer I rang the castle and asked to speak to Dick Guttman, Brosnan's publicist who was handling the *Hello!* magazine deal. He wasn't in his room, but I got his room number. When we arrived at Ashford Castle there was security everywhere. I told my friends to relax and trust me. The security guard on the main gate asked me for my name and room number. I gave Guttman's name and room number. He checked it against his list and we were in. The boys were in shock and so was I. We had just conned our way into the biggest wedding of the year.

Once inside I put on a baseball hat and glasses, as most of the security guards were from Dublin and would have known me. Derek stayed in the car, too scared to move in case we got arrested. Padraig and myself walked around the grounds and started to take photos. We even got close enough to get a photo of the marquee where the wedding was to be held the following day.

The only photo remaining of Padraig Hearns taken by me inside Pierce Brosnan's wedding. The marquee beside the lakes in Ashford Castle where the reception was held can be seen in the background

While we were taking the photos Pierce Brosnan came out of the castle and started walking towards us. We were about to be rumbled by 007 himself. He would know every guest at the wedding and we would have been caught. Thinking quickly, we hid the camera and I started checking the wires at our feet. Padraig looked at me and started doing the same. We made it look like we were electricians working at the castle and just kept our heads down until he passed. Once he went into the marquee we got out as fast as we could. It was without a doubt the cheekiest thing I have ever done.

Back in Dublin, the actress and model Liz Hurley was arriving in Dublin to launch the new Estée Lauder range. Her visit was highly un-controversial and just a stage-managed photo shoot. I was too busy interviewing Huey Morgan to attend. Huey was Andrea Corr's ex-boyfriend and the lead singer with the band the Fun Lovin' Criminals. He was back in town, and this time was caught partying with a couple of lap-dancers, a story which was much more fun than anything Liz Hurley was doing.

The Hollywood actress and star of Clueless, Alicia Silverstone learns to pull a pint of Guiness in Dublin's Gaiety Theatre during a private party

The annual Slane Castle concert in August was going to be the biggest ever. U2 were doing not just one, but two massive concerts in the venue which held 80,000 fans. The local council had allowed the second show to go ahead for just that year. Each concert sold out and had a combined crowd of 160,000 people. I got two VIP tickets from a friend, but spent the day backstage in the VIP area hiding from U2's manager Paul McGuinness, as I was sure he would throw me out if he saw me. Thankfully, he didn't see me, but I was told I looked much more suspicious in dark glasses and a baseball hat than I would have without them.

By the end of August, Bertie and Celia were in Spain. Her column in *The Mirror* had disappeared. Again, I was far more interested in Hollywood stars than in Celia. The star of *Clueless*, Alicia Silverstone, had turned up with the actor Woody Harrelson in Dublin's Gaiety Theatre, and we got some great shots of her pulling pints of Guinness behind the bar. The stars had been in town for the U2 concert and were enjoying a spot of Irish hospitality. The Oscar-winner Catherine Zeta Jones and her husband Michael Douglas also arrived in Dublin at the same time. A spot of golf in a few of Ireland's top courses was on the menu. They even managed a quick bite in a local Howth restaurant. The owner was another smart man who got a photo of himself with the Douglases and sent it to me. He got loads of publicity and I got a story. Everybody did well out of the deal yet again.

The owner of the restaurant in Howth, Co. Dublin with the Douglases during a private golfing visit couple made to Ireland

By the end of September even stories of Barry's Egan's love-life were going into the diary, and Ciara was being asked to write them. Barry, as I have said before, was in a sort-of supervisory role between Anne and me. These stories were being included in the diary despite the fact that I was working hard at getting good showbiz stories. I wrote about Tara Palmer-Tomkinson's flying into Ireland and getting €5,000 to open a furniture store.

With a clean and sober Tara Palmer Tomkinson. However, you would be mistaken in thinking I was on drugs in this photo

I also wrote about Christy Turlington's visit to Ireland to open a beauty-products shop and Posh Spice coming in for a 'Late Late Show' appearance. Plus I was getting exclusive interviews, one of which was with the 51-year-old singer Don Baker, whom the tabloids had claimed was dating an 18-year-old (he wasn't and wanted to clear up the facts).

When Ciara went on holiday I did the whole diary myself and got some great exclusives. I got the story on Madonna's plans to play Slane Castle, which she did in 2004. This time I didn't get to met her, which was fine as she is a scary girl. I also wrote about Elle

MacPherson's visit to launch her own lingerie range in Dublin's Brown Thomas. Elle was a supermodel who did what supermodels do: make money, smile, pose for the snappers and say absolutely nothing of importance whatsoever.

I was unhappy with the direction the Sindo diary was taking. There were far too many society stories and not enough showbiz. Then everything to do with my editorial issues seemed silly as events unfolded in New York. The date was September 11.

I had spent the early part of the week in Northern Ireland recording the show 'Fish out of Water' for the BBC. We were on the last day of shooting when I was getting changed in my hotel room and saw what was happening in America. It was deeply shocking. My girlfriend was in Australia and she was equally in shock. We both watched the events of the morning unfold and the World Trade Centre fall. She now had to find a new way to get home as the airline she was booked on had collapsed. I drove home to Dublin trying to pick up what I could from the radio stations in the car. The radio media were themselves still trying to find out any information they could. Since then it has become one of those days on which no matter who you ask, he or she will remember where they were on September 11, 2001.

The following week it was back to normal for the diary and myself, as we covered the Angel's Quest fashion show in the British Ambassador's residence. Alison O'Reilly, the wife of our real boss Gavin O'Reilly, son of Sir Tony O'Reilly, owner of Independent Newspapers, sat beside me. She was a charm to chat to. She was the most stunning woman in Ireland and we chatted about music and her acting career (she starred both in a Bond movie and in an Indiana Jones movie). She told me how Gavin wooed her by flying over to her when she was on the set of a movie called 'Major League 2' with Charlie Sheen. Gavin had proposed and she had said yes.

In October I went down to Cork to interview the actor Jeremy Irons, who was restoring a castle and having trouble with the natives for painting it orange. He explained that this was the colour the castle would originally have painted, and that the orange would actually look rustic in time.

The UK DJ Sara Cox was in County Wicklow to get married, and Conrad Gallagher was still just about keeping his head above water with a new restaurant on Shaftsbury Avenue in London. I went over one night to see it and ended up in the exclusive China White nightclub with the chef. A friend of mine from the *Irish Examiner*, PJ Gibbons (now the publisher of *Social and Personal* magazine) and I ended up in the back of Conrad's porsche flying around London from club to club. China White is one of those London clubs you are forever reading about in the glossy magazines. In reality, however, it's a bit of a dump. I thought it was dirty and a tad like a cheap hooker's hotel — as if I knew what a cheap hooker's hotel looked like.

A few weeks later I got a great interview with my friend Miriam Ahern. She told me that herself and Bertie Ahern were not getting divorced, ever. "I haven't the energy and he hasn't the time," she said. The story made the paper's front page and everyone was happy with it. Well, everyone, that is, except Celia Larkin, Bertie's long-suffering girlfriend, who saw herself marrying him one day.

The Oscar-nominated director and writer Jim Sheridan won €100,000 at the races with his own horse the following week. Then the actor Jonathan Rhys-Myers told me he got taken in for questioning in a North African airport when he was coming home to Ireland from his home in Morocco. He explained that the airport security had thought that he was one of Osama Bin Laden's boys, and not a nice young man from Cork, and had taken him into a dark room in the back of the airport. Thankfully, just as he was having visions of *Midnight Express*, he was released and allowed to go home.

With the Oscar nominated director Jim Sheridan at the races

By mid-October, I was out on the streets of Dublin again, trying to prove that the model Roberta Rawet from South Africa was dating some guy from the band the Hothouse Flowers. She was, and we got the photos to prove it. Lillies head office was robbed of all its takings as four men dressed as Gardaí dropped in and relieved them of all their cash.

By the end of October I was gearing up for the Sinatra ball, which I helped run with a young lady called Fiona Nagle. I had persuaded Sinead O'Connor to sing at the ball, and all I had to do now was get some more stars to appear.

I knew that Pierce Brosnan was in town filming *Evelyn*, his new movie, with the star of 'ER', Julianna Margulies, and the actor Aidan Quinn. As the ball got closer I came up with a plan. I got myself two tickets to the ball and wrote a note to both Julianna and Aidan asking them to come to the ball. However, I signed the note from Sinead O'Connor, hoping that the two stars would turn up if Sinead herself had asked them. On the night of the ball, I joked to friends that they should make space at our table in case the actors turned up, not thinking that they would. Everyone was as shocked as I was when both stars walked in to join us.

Actors Aidan Quinn and Julianna Margulies in Dublin

After I was picked up off the floor, I started to worry that Sinead would start chatting to them and they would thank her for her invitation. Thankfully, I got away with it, and we all had a wonderful night. Sinead has to be the most talented vocalist in the world and I know now why two of Hollywood's great actors wanted to see her.

In *The Mirror* newspaper on October 30, 2001, Bryan McFadden did an interview with my showbiz nemesis, Paul Martin. I had broken the story on how Bryan was set to marry his girlfriend, Kerry Katona, in Slane Castle, and Bryan wasn't happy about this. He wanted to set the record straight, and did so by talking to Paul in an interview for *The Mirror*. I kept a copy of the interview so that I could quote from it exactly. The following is what was Bryan McFadden said:

"We are not getting married in Slane, it's a load of rubbish written by Jason O'Callaghan in Dublin. The guy who wrote that is fat prat. He's a fat, bald prat. Yes, Jason, you are a fat prat. You know the way in England you have Elton John, OBE? In Ireland it's Jason O'Callaghan OFP. Overweight fat prat. He started off by saying I

was getting married in Sligo, now it's apparently Slane. The next time I'm going to Slane it will probably be for a concert."
On January 5, 2002, after a ceremony in Rathfeigh Church in County Meath, Bryan and Kerry headed off to their wedding reception in Slane Castle. Need I say more? I guess if I'm an OFP and Elton's an OBE, Bryan must be an OBL — Outright Bloody Liar.

Another interesting incident concerning the subject of marriage happened at the beginning of December when I was chasing the Tánaiste of Ireland around Dublin trying to find out if she was getting married. Mary Harney was not the ideal sex symbol, but she was big news as the second-most powerful person in the Government and next in line to the Taoiseach. So when I got news of her upcoming wedding, I found out where she was and asked her straight out did she have an announcement to make. She said no, and laughed it off.

The next week she got married in a registry office. The following day I asked her why she had lied to me. She then did what any politician would do and said "You didn't ask me was I getting married. You just asked did I have an announcement to make." So I just said the next thing that came into my mind and asked her was she pregnant. But, she said, she wasn't. However, the lads in the newsroom and the whole Sunday Indo team said it was the funniest thing they had ever heard. I must have been the only reporter in history to ask the most powerful woman in Ireland if she was pregnant.

Later that month, during a speech in the Westin hotel (where I had asked her about her pregnancy), Harney told over 500 guests about the incident and made me the butt of all her jokes. It was an interesting moment and not the type of speech I had been expecting to be a part of.

CHAPTER 12

McFADDEN THE LIAR

(JANUARY–JUNE 2002)

Bryan gives his first interview after splitting with his wife

It was January 2002 when Bryan McFadden was shown to be the liar that he is. His wedding was in Slane Castle and my story was right. Bryan's interview to *The Mirror* was full to the brim with lies. When asked about it today, no doubt he will say he was trying to protect his privacy. A big fat cheque from *OK!* magazine seemed to wash any of that privacy away in the first place. Looking back at the media hype surrounding the wedding, maybe we should have seen what was coming and how it would all end in tears for the couple.

It had all worked out for Posh Spice and David Beckham, so everyone thought maybe Bryan and Kerry would last. During the Bryan/Kerry wedding the media masses, myself included, camped outside yet another church. This time it was in the tiny village of Rathfeigh in County Meath. It was January and the depths of winter. After getting sunburn at the Beckham and Brosnan weddings, I was now getting frostbite at the McFadden wedding. I found myself trying my usual tricks to get into yet another star-stuffed wedding. The glossy magazines that had bought the rights to the day were protecting their money at all costs. It was one of the first weddings where a black tent was used to cover the car as the couple arrived at the church and made that long journey of around three feet to the front door.

Years later Bryan said that the wedding actually cost him money and if he were to go back in time he wouldn't have sold the rights to the magazine at all. He said the backlash from the press and the difficulties in dealing with the magazine's photographers stopped him enjoying the day. It was hardly a good way to start married life.

As for me, my day was spent trying to get into the church and into the reception in Slane Castle. I couldn't get near Slane, but did get up as far as the door of the church, which I managed to access via the graveyard. Sadly, I didn't get to meet the happy couple, as they used the same security people who handled all of the celebrity weddings in Ireland, and by that stage I was well known to them. I was Public Enemy Number One when it came to events like this, but I like to think that the stars would have been insulted if I hadn't tried and break into their wedding. It would have been a terrible snub for them.

Bryan and Kerry set off to honeymoon in South Africa. However, soon after they returned, the news that Bryan had been a bad boy on his stag night leaked out. A lap-dancer claimed that Bryan had not been quite the gentleman Kerry thought he had been during the drunken boys' night on the town. The details of the story are still quiet controversial, but the dancer claimed Bryan had messed around with her in a hotel room. Then, when she tried to get money out of him to keep quiet, he thought the best thing to do would be to give in to her. He couldn't have her going to the tabloids and telling the world what he had done.

In the end, even though she did not talk about what happened on the night, she did, due to a legal loophole, manage to sell her story. You see, the legal gag order said that she could not to talk about what happened on the night. This, however, did not preclude her from talking about the legal deal she had made not to talk about what happened on the night. Bryan has often said that this mistake with the lap-dancer cost him his marriage. The couple never recovered from it.

By the end of January 'Sex and the City' star Sarah Jessica Parker was in Dublin and dining in the Unicorn with her husband, actor Matthew Broderick, best known for his role in *Ferris Bueller's Day Off*. The couple settled in a cottage in Donegal owned by Broderick's family. Few know that the actor has been coming to Ireland for years and it was during a visit to his family home in the early eighties that he was involved in a car accident with his then girlfriend, Jennifer Grey, the star of the hit movie *Dirty Dancing*. The accident left a mother and daughter dead but Broderick was cleared by the Gardaí, who found that the crash had been an accident. Still it must have been extremely traumatic for everyone involved. The actor had been driving late at night and the mother and daughter were out walking when his car hit them.

On a lighter note this was also around the time that Ireland's first reality pop stars became overnight sensations. Their band was called Six, maybe due to the fact that they would be forgotten in about six weeks? When they were launched they had a huge Number 1 in the charts, with record singles sales. A while later they disappeared into history. I was given the chance to interview them first, and a meeting was arranged in a secret location (The Killiney Castle Hotel) where I was introduced to the band, who all seemed to be nice enough kids. It would have been nice to see them doing well. But, with the amount of reality TV shows churning out ready-made pop stars very few actually make it past the three-months phase in their careers.

Next on my list of things to do was an interview with Westlife's

Nicky Byrne and the Taoiseach's daughter, Georgina Ahern. Nicky told me the couple would definitely be getting married, but gave no details. It was a story that everyone was chasing. When it did come out a while later it was Louis Walsh who let it slip, this time to Eugene Masterson in the *Sunday World*, who broke the story the week after Christmas. I'm still hoping to get the story when she announces they are having their first baby. This would make Bertie a granddad. It's going to be a big scoop for whoever gets it. However, I can tell you that you will most likely read it in the *Sunday World*. The paper's main showbiz columnist, Eddie Rowley, has been at the paper since it started 25 years ago. He was smart enough to write about the all up-and-coming bands at the start of their careers and has being reaping the rewards ever since. Nicky Byrne even told me that when they are blessed with a child, Eddie would get the call before I did.

At the start of February, I heard that the supermodel Helena Christensen was in town. I found out she was doing a photo shoot in a Dublin studio. I got a photographer and "door-stepped" her, newspaper talk for basically jumping out of a bush. We got her as she left the studio and got a good shot of the supermodel in full pose exclusively for the paper. A week later photos of Michael Flatley were all over the tabloids. The dancer had put on weight since he retired and was photographed in Barbados walking on a beach with Lisa Murphy. Later that same year, after I published the photo of him with a beer-belly, he grabbed me in Lillies to show me how much weight he had lost, flexing his muscles and showing me his flat stomach. "Now, what do you have to say to that?" he said, as he put my hand on his flat stomach. I was too shocked to comment.

I met up with Bono's wife, Ali, for an interview in mid-February. She told me that after recently having her fourth child, the couple would be having no more kids and that four was enough. Laughing, she also told me how Bono would never go for the job as the President of Ireland because they would never move to a smaller house. Ali was always a total pleasure to deal with. Being the wife of the world's biggest pop star she could have played up and got away with being a total bitch, but she didn't. Celebrities around the world would do well to take a page out of her book.

On the day of my twenty-ninth birthday I wrote my first big story on the showbiz solicitors Gerald and Clodagh Kean. I guess they were Ireland's answer to Donald and Ivana Trump, and, as I had become quite good friends with the couple, they seemed to be well worth writing about. They were charming to deal with and as Gerald represented a host of stars, every time he would be out on the town some celebrity or another would be with him. From Simon Le Bon to Alan Shearer, you never knew who Gerald would turn up with to an event. For his wife's fortieth birthday, Gerald bought her a private jet and I even got to fly in it once when he took me to see a Manchester United game at Old Trafford. It was definitely one of the highlights of my career, even though many feel it was wasted on me as I had no interest in football at the time.

In March Ciara did a story on the chart-topping singer Dido and how she was a cousin of the former leader of one of Ireland's political parties, Dessie O'Malley (although I cannot see any family resemblance). The model Jodie Kidd was back in Ireland yet again, this time to promote something for one of the phone companies. It was also the month when I decided to make peace with Bono and ask him why he had me thrown out of his party at the Brit Awards. During one of our many chats he said "It was a private party and not for the press." I asked him if we could be friends and start again. He said "If you make an effort, we will make an effort." So it was agreed.

The signer Enrique Iglesias was also in town that week and hit Cruzzo's restaurant in Malahide, a restaurant Ronan Keating had booked him into. I don't think they were friends but I'm sure the record companies may have put the two of them in touch. Ronan's wife Yvonne had also been in the press that week after taking €15,000 to do a photo shoot to promote the new estate near Malahide where she and Ronan had bought their new home. Who would have thought they needed the money? It must have worked, as Westlife's Nicky Byrne and his wife bought a house in the same estate shortly afterwards.

By the end of March Conrad Gallagher's time was up and he was sacked as head chef of the restaurant in London. His last-remaining Dublin restaurant, Peacock Alley, then closed with bills of €80,000 for unpaid licence fees. At this stage it seemed as if everyone in Dublin had tired of the playboy chef.

Naomi Campbell let down the boys from Westlife at the start of April when she failed to turn up for a planned video shoot. Instead, they got in Leah Wood, daughter of Ron Wood, to save the video shoot. They were less than kind about Naomi when I talked to Bryan about the supermodel and deservedly so after what she did.

Stephen Gately, formally of Boyzone, had broken up with his long-term partner. When it had emerged that he was gay a few years earlier, Louis Walsh had been forced to admit that the stories he had been peddling during the Boyzone days about Stephen getting engaged to Emma Bunton (Baby Spice) from The Spice Girls had actually been untrue. That was just Louis's way of lying to the press to get publicity, and you really can't fault it. Look how well he has done from it.

The legendary actor Michael Caine was in town at the same time, making a movie with the comic Dylan Moran called *The Actors*. It was funny in a silly type of way.

A few weeks later Ciara went on holidays and Anne Harris brought in a friend of hers called Fiona Nagle. Although she was a friend I had worked with on the Sinatra ball, she knew she wasn't a journalist, and, from what I gathered, knew she was only doing the diary for a bit of fun.

One day the former TV presenter Mike Murphy rang me to confirm he was getting remarried. I had earlier made some enquires about the rumour that he had planned to marry his girlfriend, as he had split with his wife some years before. Mike had come forward to clear up the facts. It was an example of how a professional should work. After years on TV and radio, Mike knew how to deal with the press. He confirmed the story and even gave us a nice picture. The story was good, the photo was better and everybody went home happy.

At the start of May my Showbiz Ireland website was flying and *WHO* magazine was winding down. I was asked by John Foley, Eddie Irvine's business partner in his Dublin bars, to organise a massive party for Eddie's girlfriend's twenty-first birthday. I was sure Eddie's thirty-seventh birthday was too far away either.

In March, I had organised a huge party in Cocoon for the Showbiz Ireland website's second birthday. By then we had reached five million page impressions per month. Everyone was there, including Sinead O'Connor, all of Westlife, the former Taoiseach Albert Reynolds and Kerry McFadden, as she liked to be known then.

Sinead O'Connor joins myself and Ray Senior at ShowBizIreland.com's second bithday

Then, in a bizarre twist at around 10 o'clock at night, I got a call from a friend of mine who asked me if Jerry Bruckheimer could pop down. I had heard the name before, and after checking out who he was, realised he was the biggest producer in Hollywood. Jerry was the man who had made films such as *Top Gun*, *Flashdance*,

The Rock, *Enemy of the State* and *Pearl Harbor*, plus a host of TV shows, including 'CSI Las Vegas'. He arrived in Ireland to make the Veronica Guerin movie, and had plans to shoot a King Arthur remake in Ireland too. I found him extremely quiet and never talked to him about movies so that he wouldn't think I was trying to get him to make me famous.

Later a film friend of his in Dublin, Trish Long, told me that Jerry wasn't quiet at all and ask me what had I talked to him about. I told her I had talked about everything except movies and she said "But, that's all her ever wants to talk about!". Maybe I should have just asked him for a film role. The even funnier thing was that while we were out nobody knew who Jerry was. The fact was that if anyone in the world could make you a movie star overnight, he could. After all, he had put Tom Cruise, Ben Affleck, Will Smith and Eddie Murphy in their biggest movies to date.

Jason O'Callaghan & Ray Senior
invite you to the 2nd Birthday Party of
ShowBizIreland.com

www.ShowBizIreland.com

Time: 7.00 - 9.00pm
on Thursday 7th March 2002
in Cocoon Bar,
Hibernian Way (off Grafton Street)

Surprise Celebrity Guests

to celebrate Showbiz Ireland's
entry into the Top 10 Websites in Ireland
(with 4 million page impressions per month in 110 countries)

The ShowBizIreland.com second birthday party with guests including Westlife

Anyway, back to Eddie Irvine's girlfriend's party. We decided to have it in O'Reilly's Bar, which was also owned by Eddie and John Foley. John failed to tell Eddie I had organised the party. I didn't know this, and was very upset with Eddie for not thanking me. I wondered at the time whether he was just a rude person. Now, years later, after I have got to know him fairly well, I know that he is just a very rude person. And if you ask anyone who isn't female, young, available and stunning, they will most probably tell you the same about him.

During the party a few lap-dancers turned up with a guy I knew. The photographers went into overdrive and the headlines the following day blasted Eddie for inviting lap-dancers to his girlfriend's party. He knew nothing about them, and neither did I. They were just guests and I remember Eddie's friends had had no problems talking to them for most of the night. The whole lap-dancer thing caused a lot of trouble for me and I wasn't even getting paid for it. Then Amanda Brunker from the *Sunday World* got her photo taken with Eddie and put it in the paper after the photographer Kieran Harknett (who was working for us taking photographs on the night) gave her the shot. John Foley was very upset that Kieran had given Amanda the photo and nearly refused to pay Kieran for the job. He paid me nothing but it was the best lesson I have ever learned. Don't do anything for anyone without all the details and costs written down and agreed first.

Hollywood biggest producer Jerry Bruckheimer gets branded by ShowBizIreland.com

By the middle of 2002, times were changing. John Ryan's new newspaper and magazine had folded and the former Miss Ireland, Andrea Roche had finally settled down with her new man. His name was PJ Mansfield, and his father owned most of West Dublin. Thankfully, the effect he had on Andrea seemed to calm her down so I came to no more harm at her hands.

At the start of June the Hollywood legend Mel Brooks was in town with his wife, actress Anne Bancroft, the boy-eating older women from *The Graduate*. She was filming a remake of the hit movie *The Roman Spring of Mrs Stone*. At the same time, a young man called Royston Brady was making headlines as the next big thing on the political front. Royston and I went back a long way. When I worked in the Gresham Hotel, Royston was a duty manager. He was from a big Fianna Fáil family and had already become the Deputy Lord Mayor of Dublin by the age of 30. His brother had been made a senator by Bertie Ahern, and, according to everyone, Royston was going to run in and win in the next European elections in 2004.

By the time the elections came around, Royston was the favourite to win. His main competition was coming from Eoin Ryan, a well-seasoned Fianna Fáil TD. All the polls said Royston was a sure winner, but as the elections drew closer, it became clear that Royston knew everything about getting his photo taken and kissing babies, but apparently very little about Europe and politics. This was something of a handicap for a man who was trying to become a member of the European Parliament. A scandal also surfaced about a comment Royston had made in an interview about his father's taxi being used by those involved in the Dublin bombings back it the seventies. He refused to do any interviews or talk to the press and then refused to go on talk shows and argue about the issues affecting Europe, leaving the media and the public thinking he knew nothing about the job he was trying to get elected to. It was a disaster from start to finish.

Then when people like me who knew him tried to talk to him and get him some good press, Royston wouldn't take any phone calls and gave the election away as he refused to defend himself in public.

By the start of the summer, Bill Clinton was back in town with Bono. During a night on the town, I watched as the two of them left The Clarence Hotel and walked the streets of Dublin up to the Spy Bar in South William Street. It must have driven the secret service mad. I guess Bono and Bill just thought it was such a warm night they would walk to the bar instead of taking their cars. It was so bizarre to watch them walk the streets of Dublin as 10 secret service men, 20 Gardaí and a number of police bikes and cars followed them as they strolled casually along.

As Ireland played a range of soccer internationals, I caused a lot of embarrassment for Ireland's leading TV football pundit Eamon Dunphy. It would actually lead to him getting taken off the air temporarily.

Dunphy was to commentate on TV on an Ireland game early one Sunday morning. He failed to show up, claiming he was sick. I later discovered and wrote that on the previous evening Eamon had gone to Lillies and then Joys nightclub and had continued to party until 9am. The Sunday Indo story came out the following Saturday night. When Eamon saw I had the story on him going wild and then claiming he was sick the weekend before, he did what he does best and went on another bender. The only difference this time was that he altered his choice of clubs. On Sunday morning he showed up in RTÉ drunk and clearly suffering and was sent home. He still hasn't forgiven me.

Bono and Bill Clinton walk the streets of Dublin much to the distress of the secret service

By June 2002, Bono was back in Africa doing his thing. Michael Flatley was in Korea supporting the Irish football team at the World Cup finals. The Corrs were getting ready for yet another wedding: this time it was Caroline, who was getting married in Spain. On top of all that the news leaked out that, yet again, more stars wanted to get married in Ireland. This time it was the ex-Beatle Sir Paul McCartney and his girlfriend Heather Mills. The wedding would be held at Castle Leslie in Monaghan but even the great ex-Beatle failed to outshine the lavish wedding of Posh Spice and David Beckham, which will forever top the list of Ireland's most tacky weddings.

At the same time JP McManus, one of the former biggest shareholders in Manchester United, was hosting a massive €100,000 party for the retirement of his horse Istabraq. The horse had won the Limerick businessman a lot of money over the years and was now being put out to stud with one hell of a send off. Some people really do have more money then sense.

CHAPTER 13

NOT ALL FUN AND GAMES

(JULY–DECEMBER 2002)

Bono's wife Ali tells me about the couples plans for their 20th wedding anniversary

By July 2002 I had started to make arrangements for my future. I was planning to leave the Sunday Indo due to the fact I was not happy with how most of the stories that were going into the diary were about society people who were generally unknown to the public, while my showbiz stories were not going in at all. I got out of the website and gave my 50% of the shares to Ray, my friend and business partner. The company was costing a lot to run, what with accountants' fees, etc., and Ray didn't have a full-time job at the time. I felt that the website was his baby and he would devote more time to the site than I could. *WHO* magazine had closed up shop by this stage. Mike Hogan was not renewing contracts, and even the editor, Lisa Gaughran, who was then pregnant with her first child, was let go.

So it was time to leave the *Sunday Independent* and finish my stint as a gossip columnist, or "social diarist" as Anne called us. Times were not so easy and glamorous as one might think. Inside I was fighting against office politics, outside I was fighting against the rest of the media and the majority of stars who didn't want me to write about them. I knew people were scared of me and it started to bother me. A year earlier, Gayle and I had been put on the cover of inDublin magazine with the headline "Dublin's most dangerous". I was flattered, but the idea of being dangerous stuck in my mind and I didn't quite know if I wanted to be that person.

Work continued in July on the diary. Julia Roberts got married and Mick Devine, the chauffeur I mentioned in an earlier chapter, gave her away in LA. Michael Flatley was back in Dublin yet again, and this time he was talking about marriage with Lisa Murphy. He had come back to Ireland to ask Lisa's father for permission to marry her.

Around the same time I attended the Budweiser Derby, one of the biggest social events of the year. The former Manchester United footballer Dwight Yorke turned up and starting acting the fool with a very well-known socialite, much to her disgust. Her name was Mairead Egan and she was the stunning wife of Dave Egan, the owner of Lillies Bordello nightclub. A complaint was made to the police, and he was escorted from the event by security staff. During the week from July 7 to July 13 I was a very busy boy and was getting ready to break the biggest story of the year.

The love-life of Taoiseach Bertie Ahern had been an ongoing story in our column ever since we started to write the diary. I had regular contact with his ex-wife Miriam and I derived massive pleasure from annoying his girlfriend Celia Larkin week in, week out. This week started with a phone call from one of my sources telling me that Bertie and Celia had broken up. I had to ask Bertie Ahern in person, which I did. I approached him at a launch in Croke Park. He was quite shocked and gave me a quote that the Sunday Indo got ready to banner across its front page. It read "I'm still with Celia, at least that's who I was in bed with last night." Anne Harris and all the paper's editors were over the moon. On the Friday before the story was to be published, I got a series of calls from those close to Celia Larkin telling me the relationship was definitely over. On the Saturday morning I did a second interview with Bertie in the Burlington Hotel, where he told me they were still together but that things had changed between the couple. Of course, the main headline across the front of the paper read 'The Taoiseach tells the Double Edge about his personal life', and there was a photo of Ciara and me beside it, despite that fact that Ciara had nothing to do with the story. The front page lead story had the smaller headline 'Celia and me, the relationship has changed'.

In August, Bertie and Celia made one last attempt to persuade the country they were still a couple. They tried and tried to make people think they were going to live happily every after but it wasn't to be. Shortly after, as we had predicted, they broke up for good. Bertie would be back out socialising with Miriam within months, which was something even I didn't see coming.

Bono and his wife Ali celebrated their twentieth wedding anniversary. They returned from their home in Eze in the South of France for a party in The Clarence Hotel. Others sharing the summer-lovin' included the Irish rugby star Brian O'Driscoll who was dating the former Miss Ireland, Niamh Redmond; the singer Mary Coughlan, who was getting married to her partner Frank Bonadio; and finally, Michael Flatley, who had gone to his home in Nice to have an engagement party with Lisa Murphy. Samantha Mumba was pictured for the first time with her long-time boyfriend, Mark Henderson. Colin Farrell was back in town again for the Keith Duffy golf classic and flirting with just about anything in a dress. Eddie Irvine was denying that he had broken up with his current girlfriend Katherine Rice. Caroline Corr was having a party in the Four Seasons to celebrate her recent wedding in Spain. Actor John Hurt was talking about his split from his girlfriend Sarah Owens. We covered them all.

By September 2002 the actor Jonathan Rhys-Myers had broken up with his fiancée Cha Cha Seigne, and Andrea Corr had gone into the movies business, starring in a new film called *The Great Céilí War*, where she would met her new boyfriend Shaun Evans. Bono was partying hard around town with his best friends and Samantha

Mumba was getting a €3,000 Dior watch for doing a photo for Paul Sheeran, the jeweller. Charlize Theron and her Irish beau Stuart Townsend were planning a wedding in her home in South Africa, which they have still not got around to doing.

Some Irishmen bought The Christina O, a yacht formally owned by Jackie Kennedy's second husband, Aristotle Onassis. I didn't rush to charter it as it cost around €450,000 for a 10-day trip and more than €50 million to refit.

Later that same month I ran the Rat Pack ball with some friends. It was the first time I would sing in just under 20 years. I was 12 and in primary school when I had my first singing experience singing 'The Rose of Tralee' in front of the school. I hadn't had the nerve to sing again after that, even though I knew I could. The ball was going to be about the music of Frank Sinatra, Dean Martin and Sammy Davis Jr and would star the Dave Gold big band plus stars such as Stephen and Mikey from Boyzone, Sinead O'Carroll from B*witched, the former Eurovision winner Paul Harrington and the man with the best voice in Ireland, Jack L.

We raised over €100,000 on the night and everyone was there to support us. Everyone except Anne Harris or anyone from the Sunday Indo. The event was in aid of cancer research, and I had organised it to support the memory of my mother who had died of cancer aged 46 when I was 19 years old. The event was also held on the night of her birthday and on the year of her tenth anniversary. I sang the songs of Dean Martin and it went down a storm. I was hooked.

By October Flatley's blissful love-life as an engaged man was going pear-shaped and the word was that the engagement with Lisa was off. Bono was still enjoying nights out on the town in Dublin with his famous mates. His wife Ali was going to organise a massive fashion event in Dublin in January again. She told me all about it, but at this stage I was losing interest in everything and tiring of the media game.

By November, I was planning another charity bash, but this time I would organise it and sing at it for over 300 VIPs during Christmas week. It would be only the second time I had sung live and I wanted to do a lunch to thank all those who had supported the first Rat Pack ball. Thankfully, after constant harassment, I managed to get a plug for the lunch in my own column. Even at that, it was Ciara who wrote it.

Also around the time we started to hear about an event called The Trilogy. It was being run by the boyfriend of Bono's niece. A host of stars were expected for a celebrity tennis tournament, supermodel fashion show and star-studded concert. The organiser was called Sean Collins, who thought he knew it all. He didn't. No musical act would sign up to the event, the tennis event didn't sell well and the fashion show was the only thing that worked. In the end, the whole event lost a fortune. As for Mr Collins, he did not reappear on the social scene again.

Westlife's Nicky Byrne did another interview with me still claiming he wasn't getting married. Furthermore, he had no plans to propose to Georgina and make Bertie Ahern father of the bride. "I am not proposing this Christmas or next Christmas, I swear to you." Nicky said.
He then proposed on Christmas morning. That's the thing with stars, they all pretend to be your friend, then mislead you any chance they get. Nicky, however, is generally a good guy and I suppose the proposal was meant to be a surprise. I can't blame him for not telling me.

By mid-December 2002 the Trilogy fashion show had come and gone. The Minister for Justice Michael McDowell had forgotten his passport on his way to Brussels. Eamon Dunphy was spotted in a lap-dancing club, and Samantha Mumba had launched her own sports range with Reebok.

The week of December 15 was a sad week for the Irish media. The national press plus a host of celebrities came together for the funeral of one of Ireland's top PR men, Chris Roche. Just like my mother, Chris had died of cancer, and everyone from Michael Flatley to Gay Byrne was there to say goodbye to a great man. A story was told at his funeral about a Garth Brooks concert for which Chris had handled the publicity. The guest list had over 400 names on it. Garth Brooks turned to the promoter Jim Aiken and said that he didn't know he had that many friends in Ireland and were the guests of Jim? No, said Jim, they were guests of Chris.

A lot of things came to an end that Christmas. Amanda Byram split up with the comedian Patrick Kielty. Bertie and Celia were also finished for good. As for me, I didn't know it yet, but it would be my last Christmas with the Sunday Indo.

CHAPTER 14

CROSSING JORDAN

(JANUARY–JUNE 2003)

The glamour model Jordan, who wanted Louis Walsh to manage her pop career

It seemed to be the end of era, and looking around me at the names and places in Dublin we had spent years writing about, it wasn't hard to see why. John Ryan had no publications left and was moving to New York. Lillies was up for sale, but wouldn't actually go under the hammer for over a year. Terry Keane had moved to France. Movie-makers were worried about the Government removing the tax breaks they got to film in Ireland, so no new movies were booked in and therefore there were no stars to chase around the streets. The Spice Girls and Boyzone had both broken up and what remained was a bunch of boring, publicity-shallow B-rate stars that would never do or say anything that hadn't already been written for them on a press release.

February of 2003 brought some joy as the stories started to trickle in. Nicky and Georgina were to sell the rights of their upcoming wedding in France to *Hello!* magazine. Flatley started a war with the local council in Cork over planning permission for his new home. Eddie Irvine split with yet another girlfriend (lucky her) and we all got ready for the Special Olympics, which would be held in Ireland for the first time.

This was also the month Colin Farrell went on a date with Britney Spears and was spotted chasing Demi Moore at the same time. How does he find the energy? I made my final plans to leave the paper but ensured that I would keep them getting stories in the meantime so I could leave on a good note. I broke the story on the Irish footballer Robbie Keane finding love with a Dublin girl. She later entered Miss Ireland but didn't win, even though the papers made her a favourite. I also got the story of Madonna sending her daughter to an Irish convent school but we never heard where she was going to send her. I wonder is little Lourdes hiding somewhere in Ireland at the moment? We could always try and get the *Evening Herald* to find her but they would have to see if *The Star*, *The Sun* or *The Mirror* had it first so they could lift the story from them.

Then out of the blue I went to war with Bono again. It happened at the Irish Music Awards in March. I was in the press room when U2 came in to be interviewed. The first question was asked by a girl from the BBC and was about Northern Ireland. Bono immediately said he didn't want to talk about anything serious and asked for a lighter question. I put my hand up.

"Yes, Jason?" the rocker said. I started by saying I had read in the tabloids that Bono had bought himself a brand new penthouse in New York in the same building that John Lennon lived in. I asked the star if the story was true. Well, he went nuts. "Look, Jason," he said. "You are the only one who reads the tabloids. I'm sick of Bono and I am Bono. I don't want to read about how I live, what I spend, or anything. I'm a very lucky spoilt rock star and I'm having the best time of anybody's life but I'd appreciate if you didn't go into that."

I was sitting there in shock when he continued by breaking in on The Edge, who was answering the next question. "Actually," he said "I'd like to apologise because I said nobody reads the tabloids. I do read the tabloids. People in the tabloids are trying to cover issues I represent." With that he mentioned a string of tabloids, *The Sun*, *The Star* and *The Mirror*, each of which ran a full page the next day with the headline 'Bono backs us'. But the great man wasn't finished with me yet. He then went on to tell me that my gossip writing was not the type of thing U2 courted. They were a rock and roll band and they would stay that way as long as they didn't become celebrities.

Bono gives me that look. Pic.: Mark Doyle

We responded in our normal way by printing a huge photo of Bono appearing on the cover of *Vogue* magazine a few years earlier and saying "you can't have it both ways, Bono".

This was also the same week I wrote about the UCD fashion show and a young model that I was told was going to win Miss Ireland that summer. Her name was Rosanna Davidson and she was the daughter of the singer Chris de Burgh. She did win Miss Ireland and then became the only Irish woman ever to win Miss World. Thankfully she got her looks from her mother.

A week later I broke the story on the wedding of Ozzy Osborne's son to an Irish girl. The wedding would be in Ireland and I got all the details. The story was even lifted by Sky News. That's when you know you are on the right track. This was also the week that the great Irish actor Richard Harris died. I had only met him once, a few years before, when I was having dinner with a female friend in La Stampa in Dublin. Harris, who was well into his seventies by then, had walked past the table with his brother. He had stopped to say hello to my friend and had acted like I wasn't there. He just smiled and walked away.

Pierce Brosnan was back in Dublin for the première of his movie *Evelyn*, and we hooked up as usual for our annual interview. We chatted about him doing the next Bond movie, but he spent more time talking about doing a new movie in Ireland with the actress Julianne Moore called *Laws of Attraction*. Colin Farrell left Dublin after two weeks of parties in Renards nightclub, which is owned by the husband of his second cousin, Robbie Fox. The photographers were extremely happy to see the back of Farrell as they had spent the whole two weeks chasing him around town. Colin then attended the Oscars with his sister and a lady called Kim Bordenave. We had just done a story on her as she was having the actor's baby.

By April I was on the diary by myself again as Ciara took holidays. The flamboyant model Jordan was in town to launch another bar, and I spent the night chatting with her and Louis Walsh, who was also at the party for some reason. I think she wanted him to manage her, but he said no. I'm not sure why because he could have had a lot of fun with the press with her as his client. Miriam Ahern was taking the limelight from Celia Larkin and was now going to do a spread in *VIP* magazine, which Celia had done a year before.

April proved to be the final time we were to do the whole Bertie and Celia thing. *Ireland on Sunday* had done a splash saying that the whole thing was over for good. But then, through Bertie's PR people, a photo of the couple having dinner in Dublin was set up for us by our political correspondent so we could run a denial story. I didn't care what Bertie did at this stage. They should just have walked away instead of trying to fool everyone that they were still together.

I was kept busy. One day it was interviewing Gabriel Byrne about selling his Dublin home and moving out of Ireland for good after the sad death of his mother, the next it was chatting to the actor Jonathan Rhys-Myers about getting back with Cha Cha Seigne. The daughter of the singer and politician Dana went into modelling, which some seemed to think was ground-breaking news.

The final nail in the coffin for Bertie and Celia was the upcoming wedding of Georgina Ahern. Bertie was made to choose between Celia and Miriam. Miriam was running the wedding. Bertie attended the wedding of the then Lord Mayor of Dublin (my old friend Royston Brady) with Celia and the wedding of his daughter with Miriam. It was the end for Bertie and Celia.

Robert DeNiro and Bono outside Bono's Hotel The Clarence in Dublin. Pic.: John Dardis

In May Robert De Niro was in Dublin and on the town with Bono. Why he was in Dublin I have no idea. The boys then headed to New York to launch De Niro's Tribeca film festival. They attended the New York première of Jim Sheridan's new movie In America. It was the opening movie of the festival and later got Jim a nomination for an Oscar. Bono also took time out in New York to be father of the bride (in a way) and give the supermodel Christy Turlington away at her wedding. Bono and Turlington had been friends for a long time.

In mid-May I spent the week chasing a story that Michael O'Leary, Ireland's most eligible bachelor and Ryanair boss, was getting married. He was. By the time Sunday came around he had already issued a press release.

Brian O'Driscoll had landed the job of Captain of the Irish rugby team and had started dating the up-and-coming model Glenda Gilson. I set up the first photos of the couple during a party in Robbie Fox's Barracuda restaurant in Bray. Glenda, of course, had no objection to doing the photos. Mark Doyle did the shots and the following day they were on the cover of The Sun.

The final big event of a very eventful first six months of 2003 was the Special Olympics. Everyone got involved, and the breathtaking opening ceremony was the most amazing show I have ever seen. Colin Farrell, Muhammad Ali, Arnold Schwarzenegger, U2 and Nelson Mandela lead the ceremony and it was jaw-dropping. The biggest ever line of Riverdance dancers lined up to finish the proceedings and I felt a tear in my eye. It was truly moving.

At the end of June there came yet another highlight in my career when I made my way to Kilmainham Hospital to see Pierce Brosnan get an honorary doctorate along with the Eddie Jordan, who, like me had gone to Synge Street CBS secondary school. I stood in the background while the duo were doing press photos, but then Brosnan saw me. He made his way towards me, pushing the snappers out of his way. I started to think I was in trouble. With that,

Eddie Jordan saw what he was doing and shouted at Brosnan "Do you know that young fella too?" Both of them sandwiched me and the snappers kept saying "Jayo, what's going on here. Did you go to school with Brosnan as well?" It was flattering.

What with the Special Olympics and my day out with Brosnan, it had been a good month. However, that was all to change, as I knew I would not end the year with the Sunday Indo.

Pierce Brosnan is overjoying as I tell him how he can get real action's physique like mine. Pic.: Mark Doyle

CHAPTER 15

THE LAST DAYS OF 'THE DOUBLE EDGE'
(JULY–OCTOBER 2003)

It was the start of the summer and the whole excitement of the Special Olympics was dying down. I was writing stories about Kerry Katona's best friend nearly going into labour in Lillies, and my music career was going from strength to strength after Dennis Desmond had put my Irish Rat Pack show into the famed Olympia Theatre in Dublin for eight Friday-night slots. The show sold as well as an up-and-coming show could, with around 250 guests at each night's performance.

I then called Derek Daniels, the man behind one of Ireland's biggest modelling agencies, Assets, and the producer of the newly revamped Miss Ireland pageant. I asked Derek if I could perform at the Miss Ireland final and he said yes. So at least my music career was looking up.

I covered the wedding of Nicky Byrne and Georgina Ahern which was taking place in Paris. However, even though I was the showbiz diarist the paper sent Brendan O'Connor to cover the wedding and I got to stay in Dublin. I got a diary lead story out of all the information I had about the wedding, which was more than he got and he was in Paris.

I decided it was time to give my notice to the paper. My unhappiness was showing as my efforts in the paper were getting pushed further and further down the page. In the diary of August 10, 2003, two of Ciara's stories were about Conrad Gallagher writing a book (which he didn't do until 2005) and an ex-girlfriend of one of the Hothouse Flowers (an eighties band) getting remarried. I, on the other hand, did stories on Ronan Keating and Keith Duffy from Boyzone making up after years of fighting, and a story about Pierce Brosnan's private party in Vicar Street venue. The next week I covered the Robbie Williams concert in the

Phoenix Park. It was amazing and afterwards I interviewed Keith Duffy. He was now a star all over again with his role in Coronation Street. He told me how Robbie and he used to live together in London when they were younger and that Robbie was still the same despite the massive fame and fortune.

I give Keith Duffy a few footballing tips before a match much to his amusement

I also did one final interview with Miriam Ahern. She was very unhappy about the way her family had been treated by the press at the wedding in France of Nicky and Georgina. The wedding had been a farce in the end, with the local villagers booing the couple and photographers getting kicked by heavy-handed French police. The coverage made it sound like a riot. I was happy I hadn't been there. Kathryn Rogers, *The Star's* showbiz writer, had got into the hotel at which the wedding was taking place the night before the wedding day by booking a room. She was asked to leave the following day when she was spotted.

Eddie Irvine's friendship with his former pal and business partner John Foley seemed to have gone sour. The couple got involved in a serious of rows over their joint ownership of several bars in Dublin. John was sacked as GM of the group and the whole thing ended up in court. At the time of writing (June 2005), it is still in the courts and costing both a fortune. The only people who seem to have won are the lawyers, but both parties remain determined.

I was getting ready to hand in my notice to the *Sunday Independent* but I was finding it hard to pin down the editor, Aengus Fanning, who was avoiding me. I had a feeling he knew what I was going to do. We kept going on the diary, but yet again Anne and Ciara kept doing more and more stories about unknown people. People such as Redmond and Arabella separating? Some girl called Emma Kane getting married? Victoria Mary Clarke (a Sunday Indo writer) still being single after breaking up with Shane MacGowan a year before? Meanwhile my story about the premier of Colin Farrell's new film *Intermission* was banished to the end of the page. The final straw came when our first diary of September came out and Ciara's lead story was about a harpist marrying a political spin doctor. I wrote a letter of resignation to send to Aengus. Then came even more shocking news: before I handed in my letter to leave, I heard that Ciara had done the same. She was going to live in Italy for a year and had taken enough.

With this news, I said to myself, if they hand me Ciara's salary and let me do the diary my way, I might stay. A diary needed to be full of celebrities and not unknown socialites. My diary would be the only diary in Ireland covering the big showbiz events in both Ireland and abroad. Interviewing real stars and getting their trust by not shafting them. It would be the selling-point of the paper and make us the market leader for years, but it wasn't to be.

The Indo tried to persuade me to stay, with Aengus telling me how happy they were with the work I was doing. The most important thing, though, was that I wasn't happy with the work I was doing and had lost interest in the paper and in the column. I had loved it so much before all the politics came into it. I had to give four weeks' notice, and that meant four diaries. Both Ciara and I were to do our last diary together on October 12. I planned to go the *Evening Herald* and do a run of concerts with the Rat Pack in December, so at least money wasn't going to be an issue.

The concert promoter Dennis Desmond had put my show in his Spirit club on Abbey Street for 16 nights over the Christmas period. I was grateful to him for his help at this time in my career.

In my last few diaries I wrote about Bono buying his next-door neighbour's house in order to expand his own; Colin Farrell's return to Ireland; and Eddie Irvine's plans to sell his newly built home in Killiney for €6 million. The second-last week of the diary saw Ciara still writing about these unknown people — Fiona O'Shaughnessy marrying Declan Conlon, and a guy called David Agar marring a girl called Rachel Brown. Who were these people? Thankfully, she did one story about two famous people. The singer Elvis Costello had married Diana Krall in New York. I did Bono and Eamon Dunphy stories, with a dash of Flatley thrown in.

Then it came: after all those years, all those parties, all those scandals, all that travelling, it was over. Ciara even wrote the strip piece across the top of the diary about how sad she was to be leaving. I didn't get the chance, as I wasn't asked if I wanted to do a goodbye piece. I had publicly announced my departure two weeks before at the second Rat Pack ball in the Four Seasons, where Johnny Logan (the double Eurovision winner) and the actor Patrick Bergin had been my guests on stage.

The Sunday World and *The Phoenix* magazine wrote about my departure from the Sunday Indo. *The Phoenix* said I was leaving because of the money we were being paid. That was part of it, but it was the feeling of being undervalued that killed me. I will be forever grateful to Aengus Fanning for letting me get my foot in the door, but after that I don't think he was too bothered about what I did. As for Anne Harris? Yes, she did let me do the diary, but she made me work for every inch I got.

I felt happy but sad at the same time. It was all I had known since my days as a waiter. Thinking about everyone I had met and everywhere I had travelled make me realise that it had been a good run; but as Frank Sinatra said on his deathbed: "It's been one hell of a trip, but tell the pilot to land. I want to get off." So, I did.

CHAPTER 16

THE END OF AN ERA

(2003/2004)

At Irish Music Awards with Tom Jones, who proves that you can still have a long career in the music industry even with a goatee and dodgy Irish guy beside you. Pic.: Mark Doyle

So, it was over. After all my bitching, all my unhappiness and all the good times and perks of the job, I was now officially unemployed for the first time in my journalistic career. Don't get me wrong — I had made preparations. Dave Kenny, a friend of mine from the *Evening Herald*, had been on the phone and we had chatted about me doing just showbiz stories for them. I started straight away. As I mentioned earlier in the book, the *Evening Herald* diarist Dermott Hayes had been my hero growing up and the reason I started to do showbiz. The chance to work on the diary page he had worked on for so long was an honour for me. On top of that, working for a paper that wanted the type of stories I did about household names was so much easier, as was writing for a daily paper as opposed to having to wait until Sunday to publish and getting out-scooped by the other papers during the week. The *Evening Herald* was easy for someone like me who was used to working for the Sunday papers. I started with a story about Colin Farrell and told the tale the film director Jim Sheridan have given me at the Dublin première of his new movie *In America*. Jim told me he wanted to cast Colin in the lead role of a new movie, which was about an Irish-American political family. It sounded a tad like a movie about the Kennedy family, but Jim refused to comment when I asked him if that was the case, giving me a cheeky smile as he walked away.

Bryan McFadden gave me a story about Mark Feehily being pestered by a stalker and how the band had had to call the police to deal with the matter. Justin Timberlake was in town and made a brief appearance at Our Lady's Hospital for Sick Children in Crumlin to turn the first sod of turf for a new charity home set up by the Ronald McDonald foundation. He stayed 10 minutes and was bombarded with criticism by the press for not staying longer. Afterwards, I heard he had secretly donated €50,000 as a gift to the hospital. He also spent an additional €50,000 on Waterford Crystal as gifts for his family before leaving the country. Beyonce Knowles was also in town at the time and even got to meet Bono when he took his two daughters backstage at her concert in The Point theatre. I guess that's the best thing about having a father who is bigger than all the stars you love — when you go to a concert they want to meet you and not the other way around.

Colin Farrell made my new Herald diary again in December as I revealed he was set to have his first onscreen gay kiss in a movie called *A Home at the End of the World*. The funny thing about Farrell is that despite all the hype around him he has yet to have a blockbuster movie. Even the epic *Alexander* died at the box office.

Early December 2003 saw Eddie Irvine and his band of merry men come to Dublin to party yet again. This time around Eddie and I were friends, and with my stories now going into the Herald it was much easier for me to do big write-ups for both him and the paper. He always requested to be photographed in a paparazzi style, instead of just posing for the cameras. He would always say "Look,

I will be in at 10 and you can get the photos of me and the girls as I walk down towards the bar. I'm not posing because I feel silly doing that." This from a man who spent years posing for Ferrari as a Formula One driver. Eddie still lives up to his playboy image, and by that I mean in December it was a Russian called Olga on his arm but by the time he was back in Dublin in February Olga had become Brandon, a lingerie model from LA.

At the end of 2003 it was time to annoy Eamon Dunphy again. I became his personal stalker in order to find out if he would party hard after his short-lived television show on TV3 got axed. He failed to show up with the staff of the show on the night the show ended but my stalking paid off three nights later when I found him in a "tired and emotional" state leaving a club in the early hours of the morning and I got the photos to prove it.

2004 started with Michael Flatley coming to do a debate about boxing for the UCD Law Society. I met up with him again and took time out to apologise to his on/off girlfriend Lisa Murphy for calling her the Tallaght Temptress. As I said earlier I was told she wasn't actually from Tallaght and she hated the nickname. I love Flatley — he is a good guy and knows how to play the press. He donated his Rolls Royce to charity in early 2004 and it raised over €120,000. He was getting his autobiography written by a man called Douglas Thompson, who had written a book on Madonna. Thompson told me that he had contacted John and Moya Doherty, the couple who created Riverdance and discovered Flatley, but that they hadn't wanted to contribute to the book. I wrote the story for *The Star's* Page 3.

Ben Affleck was on the radio, talking about how he wanted to work with Jim Sheridan after he had seen Jim's movie *In America*. I robbed the story from the radio interview and this time credited the story to them.

January was also the month of the twenty-first birthday party of singer Samantha Mumba. I got an invitation to the party and started to think that I must be coming up in the world. This time I would not have to break in. When I got there, however, I found out that Joanne Byrne and Sinead Ryan of Presence PR, the company that dealt with all of Louis Walsh's acts in Ireland, had invited nearly everyone in the press. I didn't feel that special after all. The party was being covered by *Hello!* magazine and was nice but a tad relaxed. I met two of the girls from Girls Aloud plus nearly every media personality from TV and radio in Ireland. The party was not up there with the wild Bruce Willis or Eddie Irvine parties. By this stage Ronan Keating and myself were older and wiser and on good terms. He had organised a thirtieth birthday party for his wife Yvonne, but was very pissed off when Angela Phelan, the social diarist for the *Irish Independent*, ran the story on the morning of the party and spoilt the surprise for Yvonne who read it in the paper.

At the same time Shane Lynch from Boyzone had made it back onto the television in a show called 'The Games'. The show reignited interest in Boyzone. Although Ronan Keating had said he would never go back to the band, I managed to do an interview with him and he confirmed that maybe it was time for them to do one final goodbye tour. The story, however, ended up in *The Star*, as I was having issues with the *Evening Herald* at the time.

In March the showbiz world went into overdrive when Westlife announced they were having a press conference as Bryan was leaving the band. It was a stroke of luck for me that we had made up. I was set to get a bucket-load of exclusives from him.
The *Evening Herald* people were over the moon. First, we broke the story on how Bryan was going to manage a rival band to Westlife, which he had met while on his honeymoon in South Africa. Then, when I was at home one Thursday afternoon the phone rang and it was Bryan. He wanted to do one big interview to clear up everything that had gone on with Westlife and to explain the truth behind his leaving. This time he allowed us to do a photo shoot in his house as we chatted. The story appeared on Page 1 and 3. The *Evening Herald* news desk was happy and so was the Sunday Indo who took a piece of the interview and a photo we

had done and put it in the paper the day after the publication of the Herald spread. Furthermore, as both papers were part of the same publishing group, the Sunday Indo refused to pay me extra for it.

The Meteor or Irish Music Awards were held at around the same time as I interviewed Westlife about Bryan leaving. The lads didn't seemed to be too bothered about his departure. They were going to finish their new album and do their tour. The good news for them was that the fans seemed to be behind them and they would all receive more money as they didn't have to pay Bryan anymore.

As the whole Westlife thing died down, I had talks with *Ireland on Sunday* about my leaving the *Evening Herald*, where I was still writing showbiz news. *Ireland on Sunday* was being edited by Paul Drury, a former *Evening Herald* editor and a man who wanted good showbiz and gossip stories. The money they were offering was like nothing any other paper had at the time, and it would have been silly of me not to give them my best stories. For a freelancer like me, the pay per story from *Ireland on Sunday* would be at least three times what I could get from the likes of the *Evening Herald* or *The Star*.

Before I went to *Ireland on Sunday* I had one more story that I had to do for the *Evening Herald*. It was about David Keoghan, the boyfriend of Cecelia Ahern, the younger daughter of Bertie Ahern. I could not write it for *Ireland on Sunday* as David was involved in a legal dispute with the paper and he hated them. Instead I did the story for the *Evening Herald*. David had split up with Cecelia and I knew he wanted his side of the story heard in the press. I door-stepped him while he was out running and he spoke for the first time over the break-up, which had clearly upset him. The photos and story went all over the front of the *Evening Herald* and was the last story I did for them.

Ireland on Sunday was a hard paper to work for as it was very clued into the scene and had all the best and highest-paid journalists with them. You could not rehash an old story and sell it to them with a new angle. My first big story for them was about how my old friend Royston Brady had hired Bertie's ex-girlfriend Celia Larkin to work on his ill-fated European campaign. Next was a story on how the biggest film to come out of Ireland in 2003, *King Arthur*, was set to be the biggest turkey of the year, according to US critics. Next, was another Bryan and Kerry exclusive in which Bryan told me of the couple's plans to move to the UK. It took place in July at the Miss Ireland final and it was the first time I had seen him since he had lost over two stone and he was barely recognisable. He later got into trouble when the snappers took his photo smoking in the hotel at which the event was being held. Smoking had just been banned in all the indoor working areas in Ireland but Bryan didn't seem to care.

WEEKEND Herald

HANDBAGS & GLADRAGS PAGE 15

IRELAND'S EVENING NEWSPAPER SATURDAY 13 MARCH 2004 €1 VOL 3 No 11 CITY FINAL

FALL OF FERGIE'S EMPIRE ▶SEE INSIDE

HOW I CHEATED DEATH IN SPAIN ▶PAGE 4

OPENING UP: 'Leaving the band was like being freed from prison'

WESTLIFE EXCLUSIVE: BRYAN REVEALS ALL

BY JASON O'CALLAGHAN, SHOWBUSINESS CORRESPONDENT

FORMER Westlife singer Bryan McFadden has admitted he left the chart-topping band to pursue a solo singing career.

And in an exclusive interview with the *Evening Herald* he reveals that leaving the group was like being released from prison.

WANTED

"It was strange when I woke up on Wednesday. Then I knew leaving was the right thing to do as I didn't have to do anything for Westlife and I could do what I wanted to do," he said.

"It felt so good. It was like someone being released from prison. I couldn't go back then even if I wanted to. It was done."

He revealed that it took him six months to finally make up his mind to go but he denied one reason was because he and his wife Kerry are planning to become TV's new 'Richard & Judy'.

Kerry's profile has shot up spectacularly in recent weeks after she won the 'I'm A Celebrity ... Get Me Out of Here' challenge show.

"Kerry is my wife and offers did come in. But, I want to be involved in music and she wants to be on TV and that's it," he says.

SONGWRITER

"I want to be a songwriter and I dreamed of going to Eurovision to represent Ireland. Now it's something I am very proud of."

The father of two was speaking to us at his Portmarnock home last night as the remaining Westlifers turned up on the Late Late Show to perform

● TO PAGE 3

PINT?: Bryan McFadden speaks exclusively to reporter Jason O'Callaghan at his Portmarnock home *Pic by GERRY MOONEY*

Weekend Herald

▶GOODBYE TO SEX AND THE CITY: SEE P11

My exclusive in the Evening Herald *with McFadden in his house after he announced he was leaving Westlife*

Earlier in the year, while Kerry was in Australia filming the TV show 'I'm A Celebrity Get Me Outta Here', Bryan had told me one night how sad and lonely he was that they were apart. By September, when I interviewed him for the release of his first solo single, pieces started to appear in the papers that the couple were spending more and more time apart due to his relentless timetable. His new solo career had taken off and Kerry's diary, since becoming a massive star and winning the TV show, had gone into overdrive. Things were going to come to a head, and by the end of September the marriage was over.

On October 17, 2004 (my baby sister Grace's twenty-first birthday) I ended up on Dollymount Strand in Bryan's caravan doing his very first interview as a single man having split for good from his wife. He was upbeat, saying there was no one else involved on either side, and himself and Kerry would stay friends for the sake of their two children. She rang during our interview and they chatted and joked. We were on the beach because it was there that Bryan was filming the video for his second single, 'Real to Me'. He swore blind in the interview that noone else was involved, and reports that he had started to see the Australian actress and singer Delta Goodrem were completely false. He had only met her twice, he told me, and both times it was to do with their upcoming duet together.

Yet again I believed him, and two months later they were photographed together holidaying in South Africa. The same place he had gone on his honeymoon with Kerry.

CHAPTER 17

CONCLUSION

Tony Bennett, the only celebrity I have even been excited to see

So, I guess you can tell that some celebrities are not exactly generous with the truth when it comes to the press. Bono doesn't want the media to write about his personal life but does want them to cover his campaigns for Third World debt relief. He does not mind us covering his tours and albums but does mind us writing about his birthday party.

Jim Corr hates the press writing about his love-life but then has no issues dealing with the media when promoting The Corrs next album.

Bryan McFadden tells fans at concerts "Don't believe a word you read in the press. It's all lies." but then hates the media so much that he takes €1 million or so to sell the photograph rights to his wedding to a glossy magazine.

The press is a necessary evil. If it wasn't for the press, corrupt politicians, perverted priests, dodgy builders and all the nasty people in the world and the horrible things they do would go unreported, unnoticed and unpunished in society. Pop stars and actors would have no careers as they would have no way to promote their music and films.

If you want to be famous then be famous. Treat your fans and the media with the respect you get from making bucket-loads of money from them. If you want to make music and be unnoticed then be like Enya, the biggest-selling female artist in the world, or Larry Mullen from U2, neither of whom you ever read about in the press because they do not court the press. If you want to remain private then do so. Don't go to nightclubs and be caught with some girl at 4am. Don't turn up at every launch and promote your albums and films to death, then complain when someone takes your photo when you are out shopping. If you want to play the game, then play the game. Celebrities can't switch the press on or off when they want to. Tabloid journalists are some of the most enterprising people in the media because they spend their lives writing things people don't want them to write. It's all or nothing with the press.

But, do remember one thing. If you do want to be rich and famous and get behind the velvet rope that leads to money, glamour, star-studded parties, film premières and VIP clubs, remember that there will always be someone there who knows someone like me. The mobile will ring and before you know it you will be on the cover of a tabloid newspaper for the world to see. There is no use getting upset about it. After all, it's what you always wanted.

THE END